NIKOLA TESLA

FREE ENERGY
AND THE
WHITE DOVE

ABELARD PRODUCTIONS, INC.

**NIKOLA TESLA
FREE ENERGY AND THE WHITE DOVE**

First printing 1992
Special Limited Edition

© 1992 by
ABELARD PRODUCTIONS, INC.

Graphics by Cosmic Computerized Systems, Inc.

Production by Cross Country Consultants

For foreign or other reprint rights, contact:
Global Communications
P.O. Box 753
New Brunswick, NJ 08903

Contents

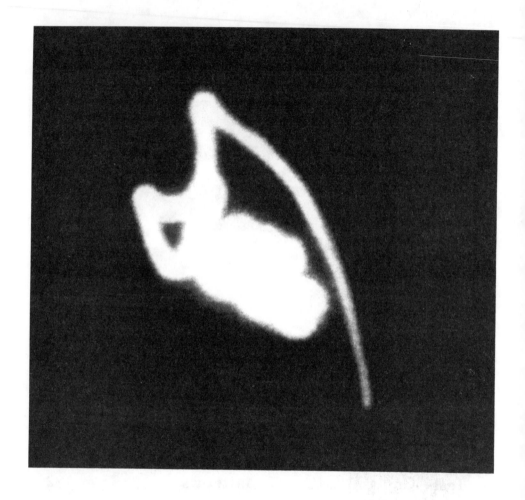

**UFO PHOTO TAKEN FROM PARKING LOT
OF THE LITTLE A'LE'INN BY TALK SHOW HOST**

This rather remarkable UFO photo was taken by Anthony J. Hilder, Radio Free America's Talk Show Host, at around 11:00 PM on February 26, 1991. The picture was taken using a Canon T50 35mm camera, sporting a 200mm telephoto lens and 1600 speed Fuji color slide film. Hilder says the photo clearly shows a saucer-like configuration with a strak caused by the rapid movement of the object.

Introduction: Free Energy– Available To All!

Let me fill you in on a few ghastly secrets:

The Persian Gulf conflict never needed to take place!

There never was a need to lose one, single, life over a war that essentially was fought over the price of a barrel of oil!

Furthermore, the truth of the matter is that the United States military now has at its disposal—and has had for quite a number of years—Top Secret circular aircraft that are capable of flying three times higher and faster than any jetfighter that is "officially" known to the public. This same aircraft can virtually dematerialize and rematerialize elsewhere in a split second, as well as hover mere inches above the ground, thus frightening the hell out of any real or potential enemy.

Perhaps not so surprisingly, this very same aircraft utilizes a form of energy that is to our current way of thinking "highly revolutionary," yet, it is so economical and readily available that the "forces that be" fear each day that it may tilt the "balance of power" out of their hands and radically change society overnight.

By now you should be curious to know what form this energy takes and where it may be obtained from. You may also wonder why you have not heard of this startling disclosure before now. The answers to such questions are very simple.

- The energy is FREE ENERGY;
- It is available all around you—from the very air itself;

• And you have not been told anything about it because there is a massive conspiracy afoot on the part of the military-industrial complex to keep its existance a closely guarded secret from the "masses of asses," who, it is felt, should remain in total ignorance so that the "corporate interests" can continue to rake in huge profits at the sake of life and limb—mainly OURS!

Many years ago, a most astute "free thinker"—a dedicated gentleman and true humanitarian—by the name of Nikola Tesla arrived on our cosmic shores in order to shape our technical and spiritual destiny. He came here from another time and another place to alert the world to the troubles that lay just ahead (World War I, World War II, and the advent of global communism). At the same time, however, he also came with "solutions" to our problems. Yet this knowledge of the Free Energy that exists all around us caused his life to become a literal hell as those in power fought tooth and nail to hush up this great truth seeker. Luckily, much of what Tesla knew is now beginning to leak out thanks to a band of a few dedicated "free spirits," determined to let the world know the truth despite all odds and obstacles continually thrown in their way. Some of these individuals—such as Otis T. Carr, Arthur H. Matthews and Howard Menger—you will be learning about as you read through the pages of this book.

Breaking Free of Gravity

For eons, men of learning have philosophised about that mysterious force that holds each and every one of us glued to the ground and prevents us from flying off into space.

Since the 17th century, man has sought to find a method to counteract gravity so that he may "fly like an Eagle" without restraint. Certainly we have various *propulsion* methods available to us today that provide this service; however, gasoline is both costly and ecologically out of harmony with the Earth. Likewise, rocket fuel is very bulky and can only be utilized in a very primitive manner as compared with the type of transportation used by other intelligent beings traveling through the depths of the universe.

You have more than likely been taught at an early age in

school that no method has ever been successfully found to defy gravity. Therefore, you will have to make a *cosmic leap* in your thinking process should you wish to learn the amazing truth about this subject. With many years in the intelligence community and while with the military, I had the opportunity to *hear things* and *see things* that you might find to be utterly shocking. I know, for example, that the government has cracked the mystery of gravity, and that since the conclusion of the Second World War some of our top scientists have been experimenting with disk-shaped aircraft that utilize various forms of what can best be described as Free Energy to travel about at what might appear to be *supernatural* speeds.

Unless you read the every increasing mass of literature on the subject in some very "sophisticated" journals, you are in all likelihood still in the dark about this matter (or should we say *anti-matter?*). Right at this very moment researchers in several countries around the world are putting their heads together in a last ditch effort to turn Newton's laws upside down and inside out.

As an example of what I am referring to, if you did not pick up the *New York Times* for December 28, 1989, you missed an important article by William J. Broad entitled *Two Men and a Gyroscope May Rewrite Newton's Law,* and therefore you would still be out of touch with the latest findings in this field. You would not have learned that "Japanese scientists have reported that small gyroscopes lose weight when spun under certain conditions, apparently in defiance of gravity. If proved correct," the article pointed out, "the findings would mark a stunning scientific advance..." The *Times* acknowledges the December 18th issue of *Physical Review Letters*, which is regarded by experts as one of the world's leading journals of physics and allied fields—as being the source for their story, pointing out that the material in this publication is "rigorously reviewed by other scientists before being accepted, and it rejects far more than it accepts."

The *Times* further states that, "Experts who have seen the report said it seemed to be based on sound research and appeared to have no obvious sources of experimental error," but being skeptical as the *Times* is prone to be, "they cautioned that other seemingly reliable reports have collapsed under close examination," whatever that may seem to mean.

Actually, the *Times* need not have added their own editorial comment for the actual researchers on this project (being conducted at the engineering faculty of Thoku University in Sendai, Japan), made no outragous boasts of their own which they could not back up, no doubt wishing to tread easy in what could be very thin, icy water. The authors of the material presented in the *Physical Review Letters*—Hideo Hayasaka and Sakae Takeuchi—did not claim to have actually defied gravity, but did readily note that their results could not "be explained by the usual theories."

Boiling down the material, the *Times* said that the "experiment looked at weight changes in spinning mechanical gryroscopes whose rotors weighted 140 and 176 grams, or 5 and 6.3 ounces. When the gyrpscopes were spun clockwise, as viewed from above, the researchers found no change in their weight. But when spun counterclockwise, they appeared to lose weight.

"The rate of the decrease was small," continues the *Times* story, "ranging up to 11-thousandths of a gram when the gyroscopes turned at 13,000 revolutions per minute. But two effects were significant. First, the weight loss increased as speed did. Second, the pattern was stronger with the larger gyroscope, indicating that the results might be applied to still larger objects.

"The Japanese scientists said the weight measurements were carried out 10 times at speeds between 3,000 and 13,000 revolutions per minute.

"In their paper, the Japanese scientists outlined an extensive search for possible sources of experimental error, including stray magnetic fields, vibrations and defects in the gyroscopes and measuring devices. For instance, they took the apparatus to a special room that was free of magnetic fields, and they tried to damp out all possible vibrations.

"They placed the gyroscopes right side up and upside down, to rule out simple gravitational effects. They also conducted the tests in a vacuum to rule out the influence of air currents, and used two different systems to measure the weight loss.

"They reported no experimental errors. They also offered no explanation for the effect and no speculation on the possibility of creating anti-gravity enginees for planes and spaceships. In their one concession to vivid language, they called the phenomenon 'extraordinary.'"

What may turn out in this feature story to be even more disquieting to those who do not wish to alter their thinking to go along with the era in which we find ourselves, is the startling disclosure that the Air Force has retained a special consultant, Dr. Robert L. Forward, who is an expert on advanced forces of propulsion, including claims of anti-gravity devices. Naturally, many of you are relatively unfamiliar with the vast volume of positive literature on this subject (and who have always been taught that an anti-gravity device is impossible in any age because it contradicts the laws of physics), will be anxious to know why the Air Force would place a scientist on their payroll who is an "expert" in something that officially— at least—is said not to exist. Furthemore, Dr. Forward says that, "The sheer volume of bogus anti-gravity claims throws doubt on the validity of the new findings. About a dozen extraordinary claims are made for rotating devices each year," he added, "and in *nearly* all of them the effect turns out to be caused by stray vibrations...Fortunately," he concluded, "this apparatus is accurate and well described. It should be easy to replicate. Most of the equipment is available in any lab, so we'll have our answer shortly (as to its true meaning)."

What Is Going On Inside *Area 51?*

If you were tuned in to Geraldo Rivera recently you might have seen an expose of Area 51, a Top Secret military instillation located just short of 150 miles north-northwest of Las Vegas. For it is here at this vast 38,500 acre military complex—watched over most closely by Swat-like teams of private, para-military security guards hired from an outside agency in total defiance of all known Constitutional laws—that something very strange has been happening on a regular basis.

According to the testimony of what may now amount to hundreds of loyal American eyewitnesses who believe in freedom of speech, the military—or *someone*—is test flying aircraft so unusual in design and behavior that they disobey completely both the laws of aerodynamics and the law of gravity. From many observers have come reports of sudden acceleration, deceleration, zigzagging motions, and 90 degree turns, indicating that these craft are dependent upon an advanced form of technology with control over gravity.

More important than the ground-level reports of sincere observers, however, are the claims of those working inside Area 51, who say that their lives were threatened when they found out what was really going on at this locale.

The first to go public was theoretical physicist Robert Lizar, who says that he was blindfolded every day upon entering the base and taken in a bus with blacked out windows to an area seven levels underground. Here he was put to work on several different craft of extraterrestrial origin, which had either been captured by the government when they crash landed, or actually given to Uncle Sam by aliens looking for official consent to abduct humans in exchange for their technology. Later, when it was learned by the military—who placed a tap on his phone—that Lazar was scared for his life and ready to talk, the brass had him drugged and hypnotized so that he would not remember what he had seen or had been asked to work on.

According to Lazar—and here is where his story gets somewhat wild— the aliens at some point actually took control of certain areas of the base (presumably the lower levels— levels five, six and seven) by using force, going so far as to eradicate some scientists who had been cooperating with them. Lazar believes that he was hired by the military to replace one of those scientists who had been "removed" from the operation. Lazar revealed in a series of interviews broadcast over Las Vegas radio and TV that the vehicles being flown over Area 51 (mostly at night, shortly before dawn) utilize a previously unknown principle of distorting space and time, "using gravity as a lens" with the power source being an anti-matter reactor powered by something the aliens brought with them called "Element 115."

From a vantage spot known a "Mail Box Road," near the town of Rachel, Nevada, a number of different types of craft have been seen by those who do not mind waiting into the wee hours and are patient enough to come to the area over and over until they, too, make an observation. Even NBC TV got into the act not so long ago when they took a news team to the area and managed to capture on video the flight of something that they acknowledged appeared to defy gravity. They identified it as being the test of an aircraft that comes under the category of a "black project," in that the military does not have to account for the project in their annual budget (billions of dollars being covered up in this manner).

So many video and still shots of these UFOs "Made in the USA" have been taken that they are not even considered controversial any longer. Entire scrapbooks have been pulled out at the local watering hole known as the Little A'Le'Inn, and shown to just about every visitor who comes through the door of the bar and restaurant, owned and operated by Joe and Pat Travis.

On February 26, 1991, one of the best shots was taken by Anthony J. Hilder, commentator for Radio Free America. The picture, reproduced on the next page, was taken by Mr. Hilder looking northwest from the parking lot of the Little A'Le'Inn. He was using a Canon T50 35mm camera sporting a 200mm telephoto lens and 1600 speed Fuji color slide film.

"What seems remarkably strange," says Hilder, "is not that the photograph of this flying phenomena was taken at its near exact moment of direction change, but rather that neither Sheriff Dahl Bradfield nor any of his deputies, who are employees of the citizenry of Lincoln County, Nevada, and who patrol the perimeter of Area 51 & S4, 365 nights a year, from the Tikeboo Valley, have ever once acknowledged to their employers ever having seen any UFOs in the skys overhead. This might cause a reasonable person to inquire who the Lincoln County Sheriffs are working for. We know that the citizens of the County are paying their salaries. And is it not the duty of the Sheriff's Department to "UNCOVER" rather than "COVER-UP" crimes being committed in the County? Rumors continue to amass about abductees being brought into the Nellis Testing Sight for medical experiments."

And if you think such rumors that are afloat regarding Area

51 are bizarre, you haven't heard anything yet, partner, as we explore through the pages of this book the amazing life of Nikola Tesla—a man from another world— and the legacy that he left for us.

Together we will discover much that is being kept secret from us, not for our own protection like some might claim, but because our lives would be better and easier if the truth about anti-gravity and UFOs were made known. Tesla knew through his heightened sixth sense that the upcoming years before the turn of the century could either be full of peace and prosperity for each one of us, or, if the Secret Government is victorious in its attempt to keep us under their thumb, there will be unending war, suffering, hunger and poverty, because this is the way in which they maintain their control over the world's population. It was for this very reason that Nikola Tesla chose the White Dove as his personal symbol of encouragement, representing freedom and personal dignity for us all. It is this hope for a better world in the stormy years just ahead that I hope to convey in *Nikola Tesla: Free Energy and The White Dove.*

Commander X
Formerly of Military Intelligence
(Now on the side of humanity)

Tesla's "Authorized" Biography

There is both an "authorized" biography to be presented on Nikola Tesla by those who knew him as merely a futuristic thinking scientist (not being familiar with his possible "extraterrestrial" roots), as well as an "unauthorized" biography that includes all the little known facts that lead us to believe he was either a "Walk-In," a time traveler from our own future, or possibly an alien who arrived here aboard a spacecraft.

If one goes to the library they will find only a few scant references to Tesla (though he obtained over one thousand patents in his name), much of which only offers us a few "vital facts" pertaining to his life and times, and not at all concentrating on his personal philosophy or humanitarian beliefs.

Out of the blue, someone recently handed me a little booklet entitled *The Story of Nikola Tesla,* researched by Wally Hjelmstad, Director of Information, Minnkota Power Cooperative, Grand Forks, North Dakota. In a very precise manner, it covers much of the "conventional" literature available on Tesla and should satisfy our need for the non-metaphysical and alternative aspects of Tesla's life that we shall ourselves approach in several chapters that lay just ahead.

• • •

This is the story of a man who truly altered the face of the earth and improved the living conditions of millions of people.

This is the story of a man who gave us a world of power and light.

13

It begins at midnight on July 9, 1856 in a tiny Croatian village now part of Yugoslavia. The name of the village was Smiljan and the name of the new-born child on that day some 112 years ago was Nikola Tesla.

His father was a Greek Orthodox minister and his mother an illiterate peasant.

It was very apparent to them even in his early childhood that Nikola was above average in intelligence. When he was but four years old he visioned that useful power could be obtained from the currents in a fast running stream. He fashioned a wheel on a shaft held by two forked sticks. When the wheel turned from the force of the water his heart leaped with joy. He would watch it by the hour, making plans to build a bigger wheel. A few years later when he saw a picture of Niagara Falls, he showed it to his father saying, "Someday I would like to harness that." And one day his wish came true.

When he was still a very young lad his fancy switched to air power. When he saw his mother fanning herself he reasoned that the fan caused a breeze just like a flapping wing of a bird or insect. He collected a number of June bugs and glued them to blades like those of a windmill. With pulleys and shafts completed, he was ready. He released the clamp he had fashioned for a brake and at once the fluttering of the June bugs' wings started his bug machine in motion.

Tesla was a frail boy, frequently ill. He was an avid reader, devouring every book he could obtain. He didn't stop with science. He avidly read history, philosophy, literature, so that by the time he completed high school in 1873, he was fluent in German, French and English.

Tesla enrolled in the Polytechnic Institute at Gratz, Austria and began immediately to devote himself to a wild fling. Gambling became his favorite pastime. There were some weekends when he gambled from Friday night until Monday morning. Nikola only played for recreation and he would always return his winnings to the respective losers. His photographic memory enabled him to remember to the penny how much each had lost. On one occasion, however, his memory failed him and he lost all his money including his next semester's tuition. This time he didn't lose, nor did he return his winnings to the losers. He returned to a self-disciplined life and never gambled again.

It was at a school in Karlovac, Russia that he saw his first demonstration of electricity. Tesla was strangely stirred by this exciting new medium. At that moment he decided to concentrate his study on physics and spend his life in exploring its mysteries.

On one rainy afternoon, he came face to face with a problem that was to torment him for six long years.

A brand-new direct-current dynamo had just arrived and was being demonstrated. The professor was demonstrating the dynamo, stressing that it was of the latest design, and that he considered it the very ultimate achievement in electrical progress.

As the professor operated the dynamo, it began to whine and sent out a shower of blue sparks, snapping and crackling above the hum of the machine.

Tesla asked the professor, "do not the sparks indicate a loss of energy?"

"Yes," said the professor, "but that is to be expected. It cannot be otherwise."

"But could we not invent a better dynamo?" asked Tesla.

The professor derided Tesla, and joined his class in laughing at the wild idea. "How would you make a dynamo without such essential pairs?" asked the professor.

"That I do not know," said Tesla, "Perhaps by using alternating current."

"Foolishness," snapped the professor. "Alternating current is useless, absolutely useless. It would be like trying to invent perpetual motion!"

And from that moment of ridicule, Tesla became possessed with the challenge of finding a way to make alternating current machines.

The challenge became an obsession. Tesla designed and redesigned motors in his head. Each failed, but brought him closer to the solution.

Still searching for the answer after he graduated, Tesla took a job as an electrician with a new telephone company in Budapest, Hungary. During his employment with this company, Tesla invented a telephone repeater which became the ancestor of today's loudspeaker. With his device a telephone conversation could be heard throughout a large room. People were horrified at the thought of their personal conversation being heard by others so the invention got nowhere. Fifty years later it made millions for others as the phonograph amplifier, and later the speakers found in all radio and television sets.

During his tenure with the telephone company, Tesla still could not forget his AC machine. Each night he returned to his room, bone-tired but unable to sleep. Tossing and turning, he carried on experiments in his mind's eye, discarding one idea for another.

Tesla had an exceptional mind—the mind of a genius. He had only to think of an object, and it seemed to appear before him. While other men spent long hours working over ideas on a drawing board, Tesla merely envisioned a drawing board. On it he could design hour after hour, much faster than by using paper and pencil. These images would be filed away in his brain, and he could recall them months or years later in exact detail.

While walking with a friend through the city parkin Budapest one day, Tesla had a vision. In his mind, he could see an iron motor spinning in a magnetic whirlwind. "This is it," he exclaimed, "a rotating magnetic field! See how smoothly it runs. No sparks. No sputtering. It works perfectly."

Tesla picked up a stick, and quickly sketched the principles of his revolutionary idea in the sandy path. What he described was a machine that produced power when fed electricity, and produced electricity when powered mechanically or by steam.

Instead of one alternating current, he would use three, each out of step with the other two. These currents, fed to windings around the stator, would create a constantly rotating magnetic field in which the rotor would spin swiftly, silently.

"With this", said Testa, jabbing at the drawing in the sand, "I will change the world."

Tesla realized the magnitude of his discovery. He rushed to Paris to present his idea to the Continental Edison Company. But their business was supplying direct current, and alternating current did not interest them.

It was in the summer of 1883 that Testa built his first induction motor. It ran exactly as he had seen it run in his imagination.

Friends encouraged Tesla to take his motor to America where they would be receptive to a new idea. Mr. Edison might even be interested. The manager of the Edison Company in Paris supplied Tesla with a letter of introduction to Edison. Tesla, lacking in funds, sold many of his old text books and set out for America, On his way to the steamship he managed to be robbed of his luggage, ticket and money before he arrived at the dock. Because of his photographic memory, he was able to recall the number on his steamship ticket, and when no one claimed the reservation he was allowed to make the journey to New York.

Nikola Tesla arrived in New York in 1884, with four cents in his pocket and a book of poetry, a paper on his thoughts on a flying machine and his letter of introduction to Edison.

A few hours after his arrival, Tesla was standing in the office of Thomas Edison. Eagerly he described his invention, the words tumbling forth, at times in French, German or Croatian. He waited breathlessly for Edison's reply.

Edison leaned back in his chair, steepled his fingers over his chest. For a long time he said nothing. Finally he shook his head and said, "Interesting."

Nikola Tesla knew his alternating current was far superior. It could travel great distances before meeting enough resistance to weaken it appreciably. And it could be stepped down, so one generating plant could furnish electricity to light a single bulb or stepped up to run huge factories.

Although Edison belittled Tesla's invention, he did offer him a job. Tesla improved on many of Edison's basic designs, and developed a small dynamo for ships.

One day he went to Edison with plans for a short-core dynamo, with double the efficiency of the best long-core dynamo.

"Perfect it," said Edison, "and there will be a bonus of $50,000 for you."

For weeks Tesla worked every day from ten in the morning until five the next morning. At last, with the task completed, he asked Edison for the promised bonus.

"My boy," said Edison, "I'm afraid you don't understand the American sense of humor."

Furious, Tesla quit his job. The only work he could find was digging ditches. Digging ditches by day and working on his many inventions at night, Tesla perfected and sold an arc lighting system that enabled him to rent a building in New York.

He pulled from the file of his brain his earlier visions and turned them into working models and machines of copper and iron. Soon he received his first historic patent. In 1888, he was granted 13 more for dynamos, motors, transformers, distributors—everything needed for an alternating current system.

It was in 1888 that Tesla was asked to give a lecture before the American Institute of Electrical Engineers. He described his system in detail, hoping someone of wealth and vision would appear to make it a reality.

That person appeared. He was George Westinghouse, a 42-year-old inventor who made a fortune developing an air brake for railroad trains.

Westinghouse, just getting started in electricity, had so much faith in the possibilities of alternating current that he paid Tesla $1,000,000 cash for the patent rights. In addition, Westinghouse agreed to pay Tesla $1.00 per horsepower royalty for all AC motors sold.

Sing Sing prison had discovered alternating current was a neat, clean disposer of condemned criminals when used in an electric chair. Edison screamed mightily that if this AC can kill bad men, it was a menace to every man, woman and child in the land. He pleaded with government officials to outlaw it. This sparked the war between Alternating Current and Direct Current, up and down the country.

This had an adverse effect on the smaller Westinghouse Company financially. The agreement made between Westinghouse and Tesla for the $1.00 per horsepower made it even more difficult. Reluctantly, George Westinghouse approached Tesla an explained his company's plight. Tesla's desire to win with his alternating current was so intense, he tore up the agreement. It is estimated that he gave up 12 million dollars in future royalties.

Once he had completed the invention, he lost interest. To waste time putting it on a commercial basis, he considered as standing still or going backwards.

It was in 1893 that Westinghouse was awarded the bid for the lighting for the Columbian Exposition at Chicago. Using Tesla's system, Westinghouse made it the electrical wonder of the world, the first world's fair in history illuminated by electricity.

During the Exposition, Tesla took a stand and demonstrated unique electrical gadgets and astounded spectators by passing hundreds of thousands of volts through his body. Sparks danced from his fingertips, igniting wads of kerosene-soaked cotton. He lit bulbs between his teeth, and lamps glowed brightly in his bare hands.

Alternating current was slowly but surely winning the Battle of the Currents, and Edison was forced to subside.

A termination of the battle between A.C. and D.C. occurred with the start of construction of the Niagara Falls power station in 1893. Westinghouse was awarded the contract, and the completion of the power house in 1895 was the supreme electrical engineering feat of the time. Alternating Current was here to stay.

Once it was established, Tesla moved on to even grander conceptions. One of the most important of these was wireless transmission, or radios. In his flair for showmanship, he invited the press and other important personages to Madison Square Garden. He installed a large tank in the center of the arena and had a radio-controlled boat floating in it. Anyone in the audience could call the maneuver for the boat and Tesla with the touch of a telegraph key would cause the boat to obey the command. The demonstration actually included two inventions, radio and robots.

Tesla's interests swung to the use of operating mechanical devices by electrical signals, transmitted to them without wires. Four years before Marconi finished his first successful wireless set, Tesla was sending radio messages from his laboratory to a point 25 miles away.

Nikola Tesla was at the height of his fame at the turn of the century. His childhood dream of harnessing Niagara Falls was a reality. His alternating current was going from Niagara Falls to Buffalo and far beyond. He had become an American citizen, and was hailed as our greatest adopted son.

Although he stuffed his designs, models and patents into flimsy cardboard boxes, he kept his citizenship papers in a vault. "They are the most important papers I possess and my greatest gift," he said.

He pioneered experiments that led to the discovery of rays, designed guided weapons and continued inventing new dynamos, transformers, condensers, airplanes, steam turbines and speedometers.

Some 20 years before scientists identified electrons, he perfected a fantastic carbon-button lamp. It was actually a cyclotron in miniature, and produced a dazzling light by the bombardment of a small button with electrons.

To further his experiments in high-frequency current, he invented the "Tesla coil" in 1891. It is the only invention still bearing his name and is the basis of every ignition and broadcasting system today.

It must be said that not all of Nikola Tesla's inventions were successful. But when he failed, he did it magnificently. Testa believed that cheap electric power would put an end to poverty. He worked out a plan for eliminating the millions of poles and insulators and the thousands of miles of copper wire needed to carry electricity from place to place.

Tesla knew the earth is electrically charged. So, he figured, why not add to this charge so that people everywhere could simply plug into the ground to receive electricity.

So, Tesla went to Colorado and built a laboratory with an 80-foot tower, topped by a 200-foot mast on which perched a large copper ball. His plan was to bombard the earth with millions of volts of electric energy, and the Colorado Springs Electric Company agreed to supply all the current he might need.

The switch was thrown, sparks leaped from the copper ball, growing quickly into awesome lightning bolts that crashed to earth. Three hundred light bulbs, many miles away, began to glow from their connection with the earth. Then the light bulbs went out. So did the lightning flashes. Tesla had burned out the largest generator west of the Mississippi.

Then Tesla went to New York and launched another venture for furnishing cheap electricity. He would broadcast it, along with weather, news and sports. J .P. Morgan and other prominent men put up $300,000 and Tesla began construction of a vast "Radio City" on Long Island. He did complete a tall tower with a huge copper dome, but ran out of funds, could find no additional backers, and abandoned the project.

In 1912, the Nobel prize for physics was offered jointly to Tesla and Edison. Although Tesla was badly in need of cash and the $20,000 share was awaiting his approval, he refused the honor. The memory of the unpaid $50,000 bonus still rankled, and he considered the placing of Edison, "a mere inventor" on a par with Tesla, "a discoverer," as an affront.

Five years later, however, friends coaxed Tesla into accepting the Thomas Edison Medal, awarded annually by the American Institute of Electrical Engineers

B. A. Behrend, a noted engineer, said in his presentation speech, "Were we to seize and eliminate from our industrial world the results of Mr. Tesla's work, the wheels of industry would cease to turn, our electric cars and trains would stop, our towns would be dark and our mills would be idle."

But this meant little to Tesla. He was already dreaming of new worlds to conquer. He envisioned cosmic-power stations, robots doing all the heavy labor, airplanes sent aloft by radio waves. He proposed running and synchronizing world clocks by radio, visualized the transmission of letters and newspapers by radio, and dreamed of inaugurating a world-wide printing system.

It has been aptly phrased that "Tesla invented tomorrow."

As the years rolled on, Nikola Tesla probed deeper and deeper into the future. What he saw, what wonderful things he invented, we will never know. He could no longer afford to build the models needed to patent them. And, until they were patented, he refused to discuss them. He became a forgotten man in the electrical age that owed him everything.

It was on the night of January 7, 1943 that Nikola Tesla

passed from the world as quietly as he had entered it. He was 86 years of age.

Tesla died in oblivion. But his heritage is all around us. It is the humming in dynamos, the singing in high tension wires, the gleam in every light bulb and neon sign in every country in the world.

Modern scientists will need another 50 years to explore the fields he actually did discover, and by that time they should be on their own.

• • •

Being that the history books tell us that Tesla was "officially" born in Yugoslavia before going on to the more esoteric facts of his life which you and I are especially interested in, it only seems fitting that we quote from an article by Kosta Dimitrijevic that appeared in the Yugoslav Monthly Magazine, *Review,* thus giving us an idea of what his early roots were like.

• • •

The name of Nikola Tesla (1856–1943), wizard of light and father of electrical engineering, is linked to around 800 inventions which have made it one of the symbols of modern civilization.

He was born into the family of an Orthodox priest in the village of Smiljan in the province of Lika, the south-western part of Croatia. He went to school in the towns of Gospic and Karlovac and continued his studies in Graz and Prague. He never graduated, however, for he was compelled to abandon his studies for financial reasons when his father died. Yet the fact that he lacked the formal qualifications of an engineer did not prevent Tesla from becoming one of the world's greatest inventors and an honorary doctor of many renowned universities.

When his application for a scholarship was turned down by the Matica Srpska Association, Tesla got himself a job through a family connection in the Telephone Exchange in Budapest. Working in the Exchange he was able to increase his technical education and as early as 1882 he invented the principle of the rotary magnetic field on which he also based his new electric motor. He then went to Paris where he further developed his concepts of the induction motor and polyphasic system while working for the Edison Continental Company.

Finding little understanding in Europe for the practical application of his inventions, Tesla went to the United States in 1884 and worked there for a while with the Edison Company. But soon he became one of Edison's main rivals, for in 1888, with the support of a few bankers, he succeeded in patenting forty of his basic inventions, which the well-known American firm, Westinghouse, purchased for one million dollars for practical application.

By his visionary and inspired invention of the principle of the rotary magnetic field and induction motor, which secured a future for his system of polyphasic and alternating currents and his other inventions—dynamos, transformers, induction coils, condensers, arc and incandescent lamps—Tesla made an invaluable contribution to the massive utilization of electrical energy for practical purposes and thus, in fact, revolutionized the world.

Once applied in practice, Tesla's inventions replaced coal, eliminated the steam engine and introduced electricity everywhere from industry to private homes, all of this to the benefit and well-being of mankind. Tesla's inventions have also been applied in medicine and, thanks to his currents, millions of people have been brought back to life. Only recently the world learned that three years before Roentgen's invention, Tesla had experimented with rays and made successful photographs of the inner parts of the human body by means of waves of a "very specific character." The American expert Beck therefore gave him due credit by declaring: "Out of the work of Nikola Tesla, Roentgen's great deed emerged."

Among Tesla's numerous patents which were not applied for practical purposes in his day was his aeroplane, capable of a vertical take-off and resembling in appearance the modern helicopter. It was only in the Second World War that radar, the concept of which was first described by Tesla in 1917, was developed. Apart from a project on the utilization of cosmic rays, Tesla published an article in 1921 under the title "The Inter-Planetary System" in which he examined the possibility of a link being established with the planets of the solar system by means of ultra-short waves. On Tesla's principle, in 1946 the first ultra-short waves were sent by radar to the moon and the sun, from where they brought back data on how far removed these were from the earth. Just how far Tesla was ahead of his time is shown also by his description, in an article, of the present-day guided missiles and rockets based on remote control, and of experiments with atomic energy, forty years before these were actually made. In this manner, Tesla's inventions have contributed, among other things, to the exploration of outer space.

Tesla—A Poet

In his youth Tesla wrote poetry, probably under his father's influence, but he never had any of his poems published. From what his friends said later, we know that he took his unpublished collection of poems with him on board the Saturnia when he left Europe for America. Contemporaries claimed that the reason why Tesla did not want to have his poems published was that they were deeply personal, expressing his innermost sentiments. He never even let himself be persuaded to read some of his verses to friends, to whom he would say: "There are those of us who sing, but there is none to listen!"

Unfinished Autobiography

That Tesla was a gifted narrator is shown by his autobiography, which was published in installments under the title, "My Inventions," in the American journal, *Electrical Experimenter*, between February and October, 1919. Since Tesla enjoyed great popularity in the States at the time of the publication of his life story, his well-written memoirs raised the circulation of this scientific journal from 26,000 to 220,000 copies, a record number at that time. But as soon as the modest and reticent author learned from the publishers what a success his autobiography was, he stopped writing it any further. This move of Tesla's merely enhanced the interest of readers, but wishing to avoid publicity the great scientist forbade the further publication of his memoirs, in spite of the enormous fees offered him.

"Faustus" and the Momentous Invention

Tesla discovered the principle of the rotary magnetic field and the new electric motor based on it in a moment of inspiration, as he was strolling in a park in Budapest and reciting to a friend parts of Goethe's Faustus. "When in a moment of inspiration I was pronouncing these words, the idea occurred to me like a flash of lightning and in a second the truth revealed itself," Tesla wrote. "With a stick I drew in the sand the diagrams, which six years later I demonstrated in a lecture before the American Institute of Electrical Engineering."

A Noble Gesture

To help his friend, the industrialist Westinghouse, who was the first to put to practical use Tesla's brilliant ideas, the famous scientist tore up a contract worth several million dollars saying: "You believed in me when no one else did; you were courageous enough to go ahead of others and to pay me a million dollars...The advantages which civilization will derive from my polyphasic system mean more to me than the money now involved...You need not be concerned any more over my fees..." By this generous act, Tesla ruined his finances to the extent that he ultimately faced poverty, while he had helped Westinghouse to extricate himself from his financial troubles and to amass a huge fortune. Many years later, when living in poverty, Tesla refused to accept a single dollar of financial assistance offered him by Westinghouse's heirs.

Tesla Declines the Nobel Prize

The entire world press carried the news in 1912 that Tesla had declined to accept the Nobel Prize for physics, which, according to the decision of the Swedish Academy, he was to share with Thomas Edison. Although in serious financial trouble, Tesla then declared: "Such a decoration means a great deal to a man. In a thousand years there will be many Nobel Prize winners. And I have four dozen papers which bear my name in technical literature...For any one of them I would give all the Nobel Prizes that will be awarded during the next several thousand years..."

Lawsuits

According to the writings of the American press, in his life-time Tesla won about twenty lawsuits against those he had sued for infringement of his patents. In fact, it was not Tesla himself, but rather his financiers who had legal action instituted on this count, for it was they who stood to gain. It was only a few months after Tesla died that the American Supreme Court passed a verdict nullifying the patents filed in the sphere of radio engineering by the Nobel Prize winner, Marconi, on the grounds that they were contained in Tesla's patents. "He was my assistant," Tesla said once in reference to Marconi. "He was thoroughly familiar with my experiments in radio engineering. He knew well that compensation of receiving waves was the basis of transmission of all signals. It was I who had laid that basis." Consequently, it is Nikola Tesla who is the father of radio engineering, and not Marconi.

Affection For Pigeons

Tesla had a great affection for pigeons. Passers-by on Fifth Avenue were familiar with the sight of the tall, bony old man in front of the Library, feeding his white and grey pets, which at his call would alight on his head and shoulders. Those which were sick or hurt he would take with him to his hotel, to look after them until they were well again.

A Yugoslav Pension

To mark Tesla's 80th birthday in 1936, an institute named after him was founded in Belgrade. Thanks to the Institute, the great inventor was granted a pension by Yugoslavia to the amount of $7,200 per annum, which he received until he died in 1943. The pension, granted him by his native country, was the only financial benefit Tesla accepted, although much larger sums had been offered him by his wealthy financier friends.

A Better Way
to the Stars

What a remarkable sight it must have been for civilian pilot Kenneth Arnold as he glanced out his cockpit window in June of 1943, and observed nine gleaming objects cascading in front of picturesque Mt. Rainier in Washington state. He later told journalists that to him the formation moved quite gracefully, resembling "saucers skipping over water," and thus the term flying saucers was born and a new age dawned.

Since that day nearly half a century ago, millions of awestruck observers from every nation—large and small— have looked up into the sky and seen with their own eyes that which our government continues to deny exists. Surely not all of these individuals, both educated and non-educated—are to be considered fools or prone to hallucination. Certainly, they must have seen something, and from the descriptions that have come to us, it is very apparent that what has been seen is something positively NOT of this time, space, or world.

Today we call these same "flying saucers," more appropriately enough UFOs. And while they remain unidentified to the majority of us, it is obvious to those who have looked closely into the matter, that they are under intelligent control, and that, furthermore, they deny the very laws of physics, bending gravity itself as if it never existed." Indeed, UFOs can come and go at their own speed and at their own pace. They can settle noiselessly into a green meadow and make themselves known to a lonely farmer, or they can out maneuver our fastest fighter planes in the twinkle of an eye.

I know for a fact—from my own involvement with the military—that the government has long been anxious to know what makes saucers tick. They have realized since the late 1940s that we are dealing with a technology that is perhaps thousands of years ahead of our feeble Earthly attempts to journey beyond the outer atmosphere of our planet and shove off into space. Under the tightest security imaginable, they have poked and probed into the matter at hand, trying to find out answers that have—for the most part—eluded them. They have called upon the best minds of this country (as well as former German scientists brought to the U.S. following World War II) to try and crack the mystery of how UFOs fly. And when someone from outside the non military-industrial complex would stumble into at least a portion of the "solution," they would always be there, ready to harass and menace, going so far as to "eliminate" or toss behind bars those who were not "cooperative" and put a definite halt to their research.

Gravity Control—Secret of the Saucers

As I started to pull this book together, I tried to think back to all the excellent articles I had read in various "limited circulation" publications pertaining to UFOs and gravity, and how the saucers manage to operate on cosmic principles that we have yet to successfully duplicate (recently, the military may have stumbled upon at least part of the secret and begun test flying their own anti-gravity craft at Area 51 in the Nevada desert).

Pulling down an old stack of Ray Palmer's *Flying Saucers* from a dusty upper book shelf, after a few minutes I was able to locate a story that had long stayed in my mind. Written by researcher Lowell Perkins, the article "Gravity Control—Secret of the Saucers," was so far ahead of its time in its approach to the problem of how UFOs fly, that I've decided to reprint the article in its entirety.

• • •

To get started, we will go into what causes gravity. It has been found that particles in the nuclei of atoms cause this force of attraction. An atom of iron without this particle is just like any other atom of iron, except that it is weightless. Yogis are said to achieve levitation by stepping up the rate of vibration of their auras. If this is true, then you simply get an object shaking fast enough, and the pull of gravity on it will be broken.

Magnetism in permanent magnets is caused by the action of electrons in their orbits. Alnico magnets are made of aluminum, nickel, cobalt, and iron. Magnets need not be made of metals in pure form. Ceramic magnets are made from barium carbonate and iron oxide.

Dr. Saxl of Tensitron, Inc., conducted an experiment which disclosed that a torque pendulum slows down in the presence of a high voltage charge. This seems to indicate a significant relationship between electricity and gravity. It is possible that the two particles are capable of interacting with each other.

As to saucers distorting the gravity field: A horse was pulled about 10 feet off of the ground by the passage of a saucer over it. The farmer holding the reins was unaffected, proving a current of air was not responsible. In another sighting, water over an area of about 250 feet was seen to be pulled up 2–3 feet by the passage of an alien spacecraft. The moon pulls on the sea like this. These craft either tap Earth's gravity field for power or have a powerful artificial gravity field of their own.

Thousands of years ago a saucer crashed on the China-Tibet boarder. The occupants wrote an account of their history on 716 discs made of an alloy of rock containing a large amount of cobalt and other metals. The inscriptions were made on spiral grooves running out from the center. The discs vibrate as if they carry an electric charge or are a part of an electronic circuit. Many believe the discs may contain a gravity field alloy.

We have now arrived at the core of this article. Some natural and man-made(?) substances have the power to distort Earth's gravity field. The normally stationary gravity particles may be caused to flow through the alloys and even through the media surrounding them. The particles could be affected by either the motion of the electrons in a different way from that in magnets, or by vibration of the molecules in unison.

Dr. Bush ran tests on various substances and found some to have a slow rate of fall, and to give off heat without either chem-

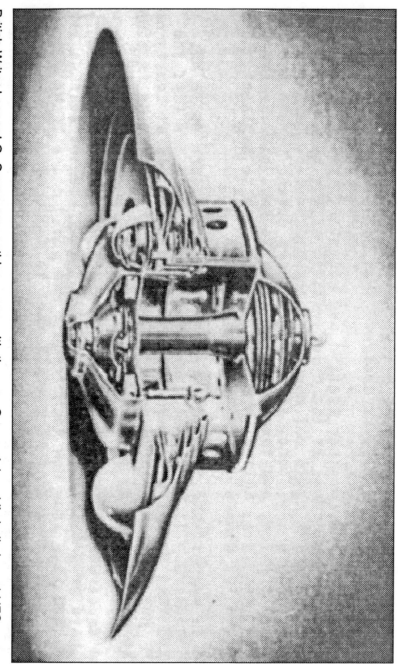

British Writer Leonard G. Cramp saw nothing wrong with the way George Adamski's bell-shaped UFOs were designed and felt they offered the best possible means of traveling any distance through space.

ical or radioactive means to account for it. I believe his report, released in the twenties, is now being ignored by the government. Two other tests for gravity field distorting substances could be to check for effects on a compass, and using a spring scale with a weight of known value to see if the reading on the weight is changed. This last test would not be too sensitive, and would work only at the site of one of the disturbed areas.

The Oregon Vortex is caused by a deposit of gravity field-affecting rock. Some effects are: compasses refuse to work, light is distorted—proven by photographs, electricity is influenced, and objects are pulled toward the center of the area. A very important item: paper scraps thrown up into the air tend to spiral as they fall. Remember the spiral grooves on the discs. Also the following:

"It is still a somewhat unsettled question as to whether the components of the great spiral conglomerates are in true revolution about the gravitational center or whether they move along the spiral arms. If we assume to act inversely as the fifth power of the distance instead of inversely as the square of the distance, we end up with spiral motion instead of elliptical or circular orbital motion." Grass, where some saucers have landed, is whirled around as if a spiraling force had been applied to it.

Rotation is definitely involved in some saucer propulsion systems. People have heard and seen rotating devices on these craft. One witness was shown a column in the center of a saucer which rotated, and was told it was the power source. He was also told that what made it work was, "the design of the column and the proper combination of the elements." The speed of rotation was in proportion to the amount of power needed. That rotating device could have been a gravity field turbine. The central column in another saucer did not rotate. There was a small disc on the top of the saucer over it, which rotated very rapidly upon take off of the ship. Very possibly it was a differently designed power plant working on the same basic principles. Ancient manuscripts in India tell of such machinery being used on earth in the past.

Some other sites where gravity field distorting rocks are found: Beulah, Colorado, at Camp Burch, which is an abandoned

Boy Scout summer camp. It is in the mountains about 30 miles west of Pueblo. Lake Wales, Florida, at Spook Hill. The earliest settlers in the area knew of this site. A circular on Spook Hill may be obtained from the Lake Wales Chamber of Commerce, P.O. Box 191-F, Lake Wales, Florida. Old timers insist that they have never seen an alligator in a nearby lake. Animals also shun the Oregon Vortex. Piercy, California, on Confusion Hill. Water is said to appear (maybe it really does) to flow uphill. Piercy is 190 miles north of San Francisco. Ruidoso Downs, New Mexico, on the edge of town. This site was investigated by the APRO and said to be faked. Santa Cruz, California, near Branciforte Drive. For a circular write: Mystery Spot, Santa Cruz, California. Another place is in the Siskiyou Mountains about 45 miles from the Oregon Vortex. England, on Snowdon mountains in North Wales. Areas of distortion of the moon's gravity field have been measured by our moon probes.

The Ringing Rocks of Pennsylvania. No distortion of the gravity field has been measured here. Listed as very interesting, these rocks ring when struck, and they also have iron and aluminum in their composition. In one sighting a piece of a crashed saucer was found to ring like a bell when struck. There is also a place in Russia where similar rocks are found. The Bucks County Historical Society, Pine and Ashland Streets, Doylestown, Pennsylvania, 18901, owns one of the sites.

UFOs Versus The Force Of Gravity

Actually, UFO researchers have long been debating how to "get off the ground" in new and better ways, to say nothing of finding more economical methods of traveling distances other than gasoline or jet fuel, the consumption of which only goes to rape our planet of its natural resources and pollute our air.

The brilliant British writer Leonard G. Cramp was far ahead of his time when he penned *Space, Gravity and the Flying Saucer* back in 1955. A member of the Interplanetary Society of England, Cramp keenly read all he could about the aerial behavior pattern of UFOs, even though most of his colleagues must certainly have scoffed at his "radical" belief in extraterrestrial craft. Cramp sincerely felt that the principles of rocketry would

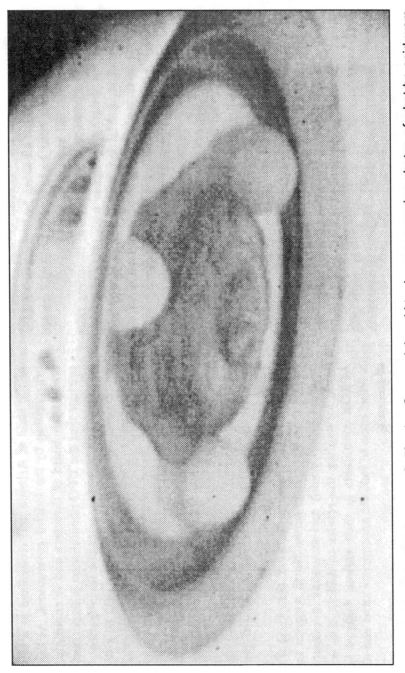

Through his 15-inch telescope, Californian George Adamski took many amazing photos of what he said were space craft complete with alien crew.

certainly never enable mankind to travel very far into space, most definitely not beyond the confines of our solar system, despite the fact that the way in which UFOs maneuvered seemed to defy the laws of gravity—their ability to make tight turns and stop in an instant are well verified.

Cramp was positive that a good percentage of all sightings must be legitimate and not hallucinations or the work of hoaxers. He was convinced that if he studied the thousands of worldwide cases hard enough he would find a "definite pattern" that would provide clues as to their means of flight.

Cramp threw himself into his self-appointed task of interviewing witnesses and compiling all the raw data he could lay his hands on. Eventually, he was certain he had an answer—somehow the occupants of the saucers had discovered a means to nullify gravity!

"If one could eliminate the pull of gravity," it was thought, "it would be possible to do many wonderful things, since, being weightless, objects could be propelled through the skies with very little force. With a method of producing anti-gravity, an object, such as a rocket, could be expelled from the Earth instead of being drawn to it."

Further research indicated that the control of gravitational forces might actually enable the occupants of these craft to make the "impossible" maneuvers without being killed by the tremendous number of "G" forces created by the right angle turns and amazing accelerations saucer sighters have witnessed. If fields of gravity could be created around a ship, it was Cramp's theory that the occupants would experience no discomfort whatsoever during such maneuvers.

Though current thinking is to ridicule the claims of such UFO contactees as the late George Adamski, Cramp was not so rash to jump to conclusions, He accepted a good portion of Adamski's claims as being legitimate, pointing out that similar craft in size and shape had been seen—and, yes, also photographed—in various widely separated locales. In fact, he went to the trouble of "dissecting" Adamski's photographs of bell-shaped saucers, and concluded that aerodynamically they would perhaps offer the best design for anti-gravity flight throughout space.

The AVRO Saucer

As far as we can tell, the military-industrial complex began designing saucer-shaped devices in the early 1950s. There are some who believe that the disk that crashed outside Roswell, New Mexico in 1947, might have been an early anti-gravity device that could have been based upon plans drawn up by Nazi scientists as far back as 1942 or 1943. This is highly debatable, as those who were at the crash site and observed the debris as well as the bodies of alien beings, certainly have never even hinted that there was anything even remotely Earthly in origin about what took place.

Almost every book on UFOs contains either a reference or a photo of the so-called AVRO saucer that was developed in Canada for the U.S. military in the mid-1950s, but which supposedly never got off the ground. The saucer—or maybe just a dummy decoy—is on display at the Army Transportation Museum in Virginia, and quite frankly it doesn't look too impressive. Supposedly, millions of dollars went into trying to get the jointly funded U.S. Air Force/U.S. Army disc to fly, with—we are told—no luck whatsoever. However, Canadian researcher Laimon A. Mitris writing in the now defunct *Saucerian* magazine, seems to have thought otherwise in his report:

The Canadian Saucer Or More "Double Talk"

The most unconventional airplane of the century made controversial newspaper headlines during the last month of 1954, leaving John Q. Public in the unknown about the future of the Canadian "Flying Saucer."

This much-talked-about aircraft seems to be puzzling not only to the saucerenthusiastic public but to the Government as well, and one wonders if the officials in Ottawa actually know what they are talking about.

I still remember the controversial statements which were made shortly after the first news of the Canadian "saucer" appeared in the press, and how certain officials made hasty amendments after they realized that they have pulled each

Though "officially" the AVRO saucer was thought to have never lifted into the air, speculation remains that the craft the public was shown was not the real McCoy, but a "dummy" that was substituted for the real thing.

other into a slowly closing trap.

A similar situation developed around the beginning of December, 1954, when C. D. Howe, minister of defense production, made several statements about the saucer-shaped aircraft while visiting in England. Today it still isn't clear just what Howels first statements, upon arrival at Southampton, really were, and who made the blunder. All I can do is to give the reader all the facts and let him or her decide if the whole matter hasn't a sort of strange smell.

According to the British newspapers, Howe made a statement that Canada has worked for 12 to 18 months on a 100-million-dollar project in order to develop the craft. Of that amount, 84 million pounds were already spent, and scientists had already taken the "saucer" beyond the drawing board stage, However the new aircraft never left the ground, and it was decided that it was not "suitable to our purpose," in Howe's words, so the project was shelved.

The next day Howe set the record straight by saying. "What I said—or what I thought I said—was that the project would have cost 100 million dollars (eventually), if carried through." He said the actual cost of the project was "perhaps $4,000,000 to $5,000,000. Further, Howe stated his doubts in regard to any flying saucers produced by any country in the world. The Canadian "saucer" was "oval-shaped with exhaust pipes, not unlike some of the drawings we have seen in magazines and newspapers."

The same day officials of the Defense Production Department announced that "not a nickel" of Federal funds was spent on this saucer project of the A.V. Roe Company at Malton. Howe's department told newspapers that as much as $10,000 was spent (this according to the *Ottawa Evening Journal*), but not by their department.

All of these statements were made, and newspaper accounts published, on December 2 and 3. One week later Patrick Nicholson, *Ottawa Northern News* correspondent, published an article, telling the puzzled public that the work on "Project Y" is continuing, regardless of the statements made by Howe in England. The article also said the expenses had been covered by A.V. Roe and the Government on a 50-50 basis.

On December 29, Howe came out with another statement, this time from Ottawa. The saucer project had been abandoned, he said, because aeronautical experts doubted whether the machine would work. The cost of the project was given as 75 million dollars this time.

So far Ottawa hasn't denied Nicholson's story, and the A.V. Roe Company has been very silent. My personal opinion is that the Canadian "Project Y" *has not been abandoned* and the work is still going on.

Howe's statement about the 12 to 18 months spent on the project is a false and misleading one. Canadians received the first news about the A.V. Roe "saucer" on Feb. 11, 1953, and at that time a wooden mockup was finished and research had been going on for quite a while.

It was known in 1953 that the cost of the project would be high but apparently that did not discourage the builders at that time. According to a *Toronto Star* reporter who broke the story, a Government scientist informed him that two years would be needed to put a prototype "saucer" in the air. Two years are gone since that statement was made, and it seems ridiculous that the project has been abandoned after several years of research and hard work.

Did it really take these gentlemen two or three years to discover that the saucer is not suitable to their purpose? They can sell the idea to many people, but not to all people....

The Mysterious Disappearance of
T. Townsend Brown

Most UFO researchers will remember T. Townsend Brown as the founder of the National Investigations Committee on Aerial Phenomena, a Washington, D.C. organization that lobbied quite heavily for congressional investigations on UFOs. NICAP—which once claimed 7,000 members—was later directed by Major Donald E. Keyhoe, a popular UFO book author, who established "inside contacts" in the nation's capitol, especially in the Pentagon, where UFO information was almost always hard to come by.

In truth, however, T. Townsend Brown was more of an in-

SPACECRAFT OF THIS AGE—USING SPACE ITSELF AS THE CATALYST FOR THE INTERCHANGEABLE FORCES OF ELECTRO-MAGNETISM AND GRAVITY

GENERATORS

CAPACITORS

COMMUTATOR

FIELD MAGNETS

FIELD COILS

INSULATORS

EQUATORIAL FIELD CORRELATOR

The OTC-X1

Trademark of OTC Enterprises Inc.

39

ventor than he was a practicing UFOlogist, more at ease at the drawing board than rifling through file folders contained unsolved UFO cases.

Radio talk show host Tom Valentine several years ago published an article in his now out of print *National Exchange* newspaper, concerning the writings of Rho Sigma, who has been involved in aerospace research for over 40 years and at the time was a Senate research consultant and member of the AIAA. Censored by publishers here in the States, Rho's important work on anti-gravity was only available in the German language. Issued as "Forschung in Fesseln" ("Research in Shackles"), he dwelt at length on the work of Brown, attempting to verify much of what the scientist had himself been trying to prove since the 1920s, mainly that "the condenser is the usable link in electro-gravitics, just as the coil is the link in electro-magnetics."

The article in the *National Exchange* pulls together Brown's research and then takes up the work of another controversial figure, John R.R. Searl, whose attempt to build a disk that would fly seems to have been successful.

• • •

The first empirical experiments by Townsend Brown had the characteristic simplicity which has marked most other great scientific advancements, and concerned the behavior of a condenser when charged with electricity.

The startling revelation was that, if placed in a free suspension with the poles horizontal, the condenser, when charged, exhibited a forward thrust toward the positive pole! A reversal caused a reversal of the direction of thrust.

Further development of the implications of this phenomenon illustrated an "antigravity" effect. When balanced on a beam balance, and then charged, the condenser moves. If the positive pole is up, the condenser moves *up* (i.e., becomes "lighter"); if the positive pole is pointed down, it moves *down* (becomes "heavier").

These two simple experiments demonstrate what is now known as the Biefeld-Brown effect. To the best of our knowledge, it is the first method known as affecting a gravitational field by electrical means, and may contain the seeds for the control of gravity by Mankind.

The intensity of this effect is determined by five factors.

1. The separation of the plates of the condenser—closer plates, greater effect.

2. The higher the "K" factor, the greater the effect. ("K" is a measure of the ability of a material to store electric energy in the form of elastic stress.

3. The greater the area of the condenser plates, the greater the effect.

4. The greater the voltage (potential) difference between the plates, the greater the effect.

5. The greater the mass of the material between the plates (dielectric), the greater the effect.

It is this last point which is inexplicable from the electromagnetic viewpoint, and which provides the connection with gravitation.

On the basis of further experimental work, in 1926 Townsend Brown described what he called a "space car"—a method of flight presented for experiment while motor-propelled planes were yet in a very primitive stage. Further, if we consider that thrust is produced with no moving parts, we could conjecture that control of such a mechanism, or vehicle, could be possible merely by governing the direction and magnitude of the polarities surrounding the object.

Knowing that the "saucer" always moves toward its positive pole, control is accomplished simply by varying the orientation of the positive charge. That is, by switching charges, rather than by dynamic control surfaces. The direction of movement would be a vector sum (added average) of the direction and amount of negative and positive charges acting on such a body.

By experimentation, Brown had developed an electrostatic propulsion method which was probably on a scale model going around a stationary pole. (Pat. No. 2,949,550). There seemed to be no limit to the speed possible, when run in a vacuum, and the machine had to be shut off before it developed enough inertia to fly apart under those conditions.

There is a good deal of evidence that some UFOs are vehicles using a form of high voltage gravity control similar to the "Biefield-Brown" effect. Some clues from UFO reports are given next:

"...Descriptions show a range of speeds from stationary hovering to speeds greater than present day rockets can deliver. Changes in rate of motion, direction, and the resultant stresses seem beyond the capabilities of any vehicles we know of today, operating within our currently-accepted framework of Newtonian physics. The accelerations, within this system of thought, would im- pose impossible stresses on any occupants." Actually, no stresses would be felt, since "...crafts, occupants, and load respond equally to the wave-like distortion of the local gravitational field as a unit."

Reports of night sightings describe a glow, usually blue or violet color, around the periphery of the object. Physicists have noted that such a glow is one characteristic of a very high voltage electrical discharge.

Description of shapes and performance seems to indicate a complete disregard of currently understood aerodynamic principles. The objects seem to be independent of the fluid (air—in some cases—water) thru which they move. They seem to need no specially formed surfaces to interact dynamically with the fluid to generate pressure differences, and thus, "lift."

"The ionized air generated by the positive pole ahead of the disc would tend to create a partial vacuum—sort of a 'buffer zone' permitting movement of the air out of the way of the moving object (which we conjecture is being driven by an altered electrostatic field interacting with earth's gravitational field in some way.) *It needs no air for lift.*"

Throughout the text a number of useful articles and other references are listed for those wishing to investigate more deeply.

The next section deals with natural and induced variations in the gravitational constant, in more detail. Dr. Erwin J. Saxl set up an extremely precise system for testing the gravitational constant under dynamic conditions. Using a light beam mid-photocell, he measured with microsecond accuracy the time required for a pendulum to swing over a certain arc. Each time the pendulum was given exactly the same starting impulse, but the period of swing varied. With all other factors held constant, the force of gravity had to be the variable. Dr. Saxl then charged the pendulum with electricity and got much bigger variations. Repeated tests have confirmed that a positively charged pendulum takes longer to swing through its arc than a negatively charged one.

John R.R. Searl

In 1949, John R.R. Searl noticed that a small EMF is produced by spinning metal parts in electrical motors and generators. The negative charge accumulates towards the outside, and the positive towards the axis of rotation.

"...His conclusions were that free electrons in the metal were spun out by centrifugal force, a centripetal force being produced by the static field in the metal. He decided to build a generator based on the principle. It had a segmented rotor disc, passing through electromagnets at its periphery. The electromagnets were energized from the rotor, and were intended to boost the EMF."

By 1952, the first generator had been constructed and was about three feet in diameter. It was tested in the open by Searl and a friend. The armature was set in motion by a small engine. The device produced the expected electrical power, but an unexpectedly high potential. At relatively low armature speeds a potential of the order of 10^5 volts was produced, as indicated by the static effects on near objects. A characteristic crackling and the smell of ozone supported the conclusion.

The really unexpected then occurred. While still speeding up, the generator lifted and rose to a height of some fifty feet, breaking the union between itself and the engine. Here it stayed for a while, still speeding up, and surrounded itself with a pink halo. The indicated ionization of the air was at a much reduced pressure of about 10^3 mm Hg. More interesting was the side effect; it caused local radio receivers to go on of their own accord! This could have been due to ionizing discharge or electromagnetic induction. Finally, and perhaps thankfully, the whole generator accelerated at a fantastic rate and is thought to have gone off into space. Since that day, Searl and others have made some ten or more small flying crafts, some of which have been similarly lost, and developed a form of control. Larger craft have also been built—some 12 ft., and two 30 ft. in diameter. The antics of his machines have given rise to much speculation as to the nature and origin of so-called "flying saucers."

"...The ultra-high potential produced by the Searl ring generator being that much greater than the ionization potential causes ionic breakdown of the air at some feet from the craft skin, as this acts as the positive electrode. The negative side of the generator is connected to the periphery of the disc and is closed from the skin. The field at the negative terminal loses electrons and the resulting ions are repelled away from the terminal with high acceleration. The electrons pass through the generator, constituting the current in the generator and provide the charge at the negative terminal to produce negative ions in the air near the rim. The craft, therefore, is enveloped in a vacuum.

"In ordinary high voltage generators, maximum potential is limited by the ionized breakdown of the air. Flashover occurs and the accumulated energy is lost. The geometry and the arrangement of the field coils in the Searl generator is such that flashover is eliminated until the thing is in a vacuum and flashover is then impossible. Energy is required to build up the potential and initially has to be supplied from an external source. As the vacuum layer increases about the craft, less energy is required to maintain the potential. The generator soon reaches a potential where the Searl Effect takes place, and the device produces its own energy along with the levitation phenomenon. On the basis of the theory, at this potential the stress on the space "fabric" cannot be equalized by flowing magnetism (current flow) through the air and craft as a circuit. The space fabric breaks down to provide the generator, which reinforces the field."

The generator then must set up an *ether flow or flux* along the lines of the electric field as is conventionally represented. The direction of ether flow is, however, in at the positive and out at the negative. This is deduced from the Schappeller theory.

44

The type field and the net effect of the craft field plus the earth's gravitational field gives rise to a condition where the *ether density* below the craft is higher than that above it. The craft therefore is strongly repelled away from the planet and to stop it from shooting off into space the field of the craft must be intentionally perturbed or limited. In the drive condition, the craft is shot out of the earth like a wet orange-pit from between the fingers. The acceleration is enormous, but since all matter associated with the craft is linked with the field, no distortion of any part, including passengers if any, occurs.

The limit to the speed is unknown, but since the craft has no inertia, there is possibly no limit as we know it. Conventionally, it would be safe to say, however, that the limit should be below the speed of light. Above this speed too much is unknown to take any risk, but since the craft carries its own space with it, in a sense the theory of relativity is inapplicable! (Another way to say it is that the craft does not travel *through* space, but *past* it!)

The rocket principle is relatively crude and has been developed very little since the German V-2. It certainly has been surrounded by some very clever ancillary equipment. But the fact still remains that the rocket is the end product of war effort and reflects the thinking of men of the Earth, not of the Universe.

The Searl craft can not be used to deliver bombs, since they cannot be released from the field of the craft. Also it is suspected that the energy precipitation quietly reduces unstable elements to a stable state and so nuclear bombs become useless. (The research on this is yet to be done.)

The early work of Albert Einstein is often cited by people attempting to discard the possibility of "ether" or gravity control. However, it should be remembered that Einstein lived a good 40 years after publishing his relativity theories, and very little of his later work is available, let alone publicized.

In an August, '76 letter to this reporter, Rho Sigma said:

"...The point is, our textbooks are *incorrect*. Einstein reversed himself in the question of the ether towards the end of his life, but his *changed* opinion would have nullified some of his previous theories on the books, and this was impossible for the

PR men who attempted to present Einstein as the Universal Genius, which he was not. A mathematical genius, yes. But even Einstein was a mortal like everybody else too. Fallible and subject to errors. Since we have, in science at least, abandoned GOD, he had to be replaced by people like Einstein. Only by studying the original source material (in this case in German, since Einstein was 51 years in Germany and Switzerland, German speaking countries), can one come to a fair comparison between textbook claims and the real facts. The physical proof is here..."

• • •

Frankly speaking, nobody seems to know the whereabouts of either Brown or Searl today if, indeed, they are still alive. Though neither gentleman would be particularly young, I learned through my "sources" that both were repeatedly harassed because they were trying to harness a new form of energy that would make the world a better place to live in and all of us live more comfortably without as much stress or strain as we have to endure on a daily basis in order to pay our electric bill, buy gas or travel to those wonderful places many of us can just dream about because of the cost involved.

It was Tesla's dream to make this source of energy available to all for next to nothing (as he wanted hardly anything for himself). As we can see in the following chapters, there are—thank God—still men and women around today who want to see Tesla's dream become a reality.

Tesla Was Not An Earthman!

Every so often—perhaps not more than a dozen times in one century—does an individual step forth who possesses the intellect to stand out among millions as a person of fortitude, high moral standing and humanitarian principles. Nikola Tesla could almost be put into a classification by himself. For not only was he a person of brilliance, but he managed to muster the courage to take on the establishment and not bend in the wake of pressure or even tremendous personal financial hardships.

For a historical overview of Tesla inventions and his contribution to scientific principles that actually enhanced the lives of all humanity, there have already been many reference books published that one can borrow at the library or buy from several of the mail order publishing companies that specialize in the technical aspects of his work. A good number of them are quite "lofty" and ponderous and have to be gone through very carefully to gleam even the slightest bit of metaphysical knowledge. In fact, there are only a handful of people who were familiar with Tesla's true origins and background, which are a lot more "fantastic" than we have been led to believe through text books and scholarly references.

Margaret Storm of Baltimore has probably done the most research of anyone on Tesla's private life, looking into his background and spending time with the limited number of individuals who knew Tesla in a personal basis (and they were few and far between). A number of years ago, Storm put together her notes into a self published manual called *Return of the Dove* which unfortunately never received wide distribution outside of a small circle of New Agers, though all those who read this manuscript (printed in green ink to lift ones vibrations) proclaim it as a major work of art for those interested in becoming Light Workers on this planet and facing off against the forces of darkness who surround us and threaten to zap our ability to make the planet a more perfect place.

Though it would have been easy to rewrite Storm's material and pass it off as our own (since it has been almost totally forgotten by others), it would not be ethical, and after all "ethics" is at least partly what we who are of the Light stand for in our daily battle against those who would threaten our every personal freedom. So here we now turn our pages over to the words of this very courageous woman who will reveal to us a great deal about a very remarkable man.

• • •

Nikola Tesla was not an earthman. The space people have stated that a male child was born on board a space ship which was on a flight from Venus to the earth in July, 1856. The little boy was called Nikola. The ship landed at midnight. between July 9 and 10, in a remote mountain province in what is now Yugoslavia. There, according to arrangements, the child was placed in the care of a good man and his wife, the Rev. Milutin and Djouka Telsa.

The space people released this information in 1947 to Arthur H. Matthews of Quebec, Canada, an electrical engineer who from boyhood was closely associated with Tesla.

In 1944, a year after the death of Tesla, the late John J. O'Neill, then science editor of the *New York Herald-Tribune,* wrote an excellent story of Tesla's life and work, entitled *Prodigal Genius.* As a reporter O'Neill frequently interviewed Tesla and had the greatest respect for the superman. But O'Neill lacked the occult understanding necessary to correctly interpret the extraordinary powers which set Tesla apart from this world. O'Neill made the common error of assuming that Tesla had died as do ordinary mortals: that his work was finished, and that he left no disciples.

O'Neill could not have been more mistaken. In the first place Tesla was not a mortal according to earth standards: being a Venusian he is now able to work on earth in his subtle body with far greater facility than when in his physical body. Tesla carefully trained certain disciples to continue his physical plane work under his supervision after he had shed his physical body.

He entrusted Arthur H. Matthews of Canada with many tasks, at least two of which are of vital current interest—the Tesla interplanetary communications set and the Tesla anti-war machine.

Mr. Matthews built a model Tesla set for interplanetary communications in 1947 and has operated it successfully since. However, he has tuned in only on space ships thus far, for the set has a limited range. He is now engaged in building a more elaborate set, and will be able to speak more freely of it since he is incorporating many of his own inventive ideas in it. The original design was given to him in confidence by Tesla and he naturally does not intend to violate that confidence.

Mr. Matthews has the complete design for the anti-war machine ready and waiting for any nation which has the courage to use it. Tesla designed the anti-war machine in 1935, but Mr. Matthews has worked on it constantly since, incorporating in it many major improvements.

Another disciple who was specially trained by Tesla is Otis T. Carr, of Baltimore, Maryland. Carr has recently invented free-energy devices capable of powering anything from a hearing aid to a spaceship. Carr was studying art in New York and working in a hotel package room to support himself. Tesla, who was not only completely telepathic but also in touch with the Christ Forces on the Inner Planes, lived in the hotel where Carr was employed. Tesla came straight to his young disciple, asked him to buy four pounds of unsalted peanuts and deliver them to his suite. From this beginning. Carr was trained by Tesla over a period of three years in almost daily conversations that always started with the peanut delivery. The peanuts were for the New York pigeons which Tesla so loved.

The remarkable achievements of both Matthews and Carr are covered in later chapters of this book. But it may be said here that Tesla is in no sense a disembodied spirit seeking to communicate with disciples and guiding them from the astral plane. Mediums who engage, for profit of course, in receiving messages from the astral plane have tried with vim and with vigor to drum up trade via the spirit or ghost of Tesla. But Tesla is not a ghost, nor did he stand a ghost of a chance of being a ghost. Tesla was an Adept, an Initiate, a Venusian. He was at all times earth-free; he was never earthbound.

Naturally, Tesla did not go around bragging about these matters. But when he did meet up with a server of the Light, Tesla lost no time in engaging in a good talk. Both Matthews and Carr have carried out Tesla's work since 1943 without the slightest difficulty. When asked how best to approach: The work of Tesla, how to understand his discoveries, both Matthews and Carr have a standard answer: "If you wish to understand Tesla you must attune your mind to God."

Tesla and his Twin Ray, the White Dove who was his constant companion on earth, are now working in the scientific department of Shamballa. and they do overshadow disciples. But it should be clearly understood that this overshadowing process, when conducted by an Initiate, is in no sense related to any type of psychism or mediumship. Every initiate overshadows disciples; otherwise there would be no point in evolution if the higher energies could not in some manner direct lower energies. Every initiate must have disciples in the world of form. Disciples are called upon to operate typewriters, design machinery and do all the other chores of the workaday world. A disciple is an outpost of consciousness for an Adept.

Many persons who worked for Tesla, or who were associated with him closely, as was John J. O'Neill, have expressed disappointment that Tesla did not leave a heritage of great scientific secrets which could be explored, and, of course exploited. But, Tesla, the Venusian, had no secrets. Only earth people are greedy enough and stupid enough to have secrets.

The visitors from other planets who fly through the earth's atmosphere daily, have no secrets either. They have a message: Love ye one another. But earth people have successfully ignored that message for at least 2,000 years, and they might go right on ignoring it save for New Age developments based on application of universal Law. Such application was the clue to all of Tesla's achievements. He was a discoverer, not a mere inventor.

There seems to be no record of Tesla revealing his identity as a Venusian during his earth life. But when the announcement of this fact was made to Mr. Matthews by the space people it did not come as a surprise in most quarters, because by then it was generally known that at least ten million people from other planets had been infiltrated into the earth's population. It had long been known that Masters of Wisdom, down through the centuries, were volunteers from other worlds. But it seemed doubtful, for a time, that Tesla himself had been personally aware of his origin during his physical plane life on earth.

However, it now appears that he did understand his mission, which was actually to prepare the planet earth for the space age. The fact that he told Otis T. Carr so much about other planets indicates that he was quite familiar with the subject. He frankly told Carr that he, Carr, was destined to explore space. Tesla also gave Mr. Matthews the design for the interplanetary communications set in 1938, another clear indication that Tesla knew that other planets were inhabited, and he obviously knew they possessed spaceships. He told Mr. Matthews that the set should be built in a few years after 1938, at which time spaceships from other worlds would approach the earth.

Tesla never married, and never had any romantic attachments or even close friendships with either men or women, except in certain cases where the bond was one of discipleship or where some useful purpose would be served for the benefit of humanity. Tesla not only lived alone in hotels, but he lived behind locked doors. Only occasionally was a maid permitted to enter his room to clean it. However, Otis T. Carr, over a period of three years, was his daily visitor and Tesla explained to Carr that visitors were not normally allowed because, coming into his suite from the harsh, outside world, they immediately lowered the vibrations in the rooms in which Tesla had to live and work and commune with his Creator.

Mr. Carr has explained that often, when he came to Tesla's suite, bringing the four pounds of unsalted peanuts, Tesla would ask him to just sit down and relax for an hour or more. Not a word would be spoken between the two men. Yet when Carr rose to leave he would feel refreshed and inspired. The vibrations in the room had done the necessary work, attuning and purifying his four lower bodies.

Tesla had another trusted friend in the person of Boris De Tanko, a New York publisher. Mr. De Tanko has related how, Saturday after Saturday, he used to meet Tesla for luncheon at the old Hotel Brevoort on lower Fifth Avenue, a place famous for its fine French cuisine. Mr. De Tanko always found these luncheon visits highly inspiring, though unusual in some respects. He said that often the two of them sat together at the table in complete silence for well over an hour; finally Tesla would speak, and then the illuminating conversation would flow like molten gold.

Both Mr. Matthews and Mr. Carr received from Tesla a great deal of confidential information about future world conditions and developments concerning the emergence of the New Age civilization. Most of this information had to do with space, with space ships, space people, and interplanetary communications.

When Tesla shed his physical body in 1943, it was apparent that he was leaving the physical plane of manifest appearances to enter into more subtle vibrations: vibrations which were invisible to the average man. These vibrations were not invisible to Tesla; he was completely clairvoyant, clairaudient and telepathic, as is any Adept. Again it must be stressed that this type of clarity has nothing whatever to do with mediumship or psychism. The latter belongs to the animal kingdom. Tesla was never really at home on the physical plane, dealing with matter in its harshest state; in the subtle worlds he was completely free. Yet for 87 of the most difficult years ever visited upon this planet, Tesla carried on his work like the great gentlemen he was.

In retrospect the pattern of his physical sojourn in the world of form, which seemed so complex to writers like Tom J. O'Neill, emerges in simple clarity. Tesla had obviously agreed to come to the earth as a volunteer worker to assist in launching the New Age which he knew to be synonymous with the Space Age. It is perfectly apparent that Ascended Master Saint Germain had to bring in people from other planets, people with knowledge of outer space conditions, to handle the major aspects of the planned program.

Tesla was designated to work on the third Ray of Love in Action, for that is the Ray which supplies our atmosphere with electricity. The first three major Rays form the three aspects of God as defined by major religions; the four minor Rays provide what we recognize as God's attributes. Christianity correctly defines the first three Rays as a Trinity, representing the Father, the Son, and the Holy Spirit.

The first or Father aspect is derived from the Ray of Power and Purpose; the second, the Son or sun aspect, is the Ray of Illumination and Wisdom, leading to Intelligent Love-in-Action, or the third Ray. Originally, we were all Sons of God or Sparks from the Great Central Sun of the galaxy. From the strictly scientific point of view the first three Rays provide life, light, and electricity to this planet.

The fourth Ray of Purity leads man through conflict to harmony. The fifth Ray is that of concrete science and knowledge and provides the world of form with an understandable functional basis. The sixth Ray energizes all of man's ideals and ideologies. whether wise or foolish. During the Piscean Age it led to the rise of Christianity and churchianity, and to all sorts of experimental economic and political systems. Then follows the seventh Ray, now in manifestation; the Ray which is now being called into action to transmute and release mankind from all past errors accumulated during nineteen million years of struggle since the laggards came.

At the present time, and for centuries past, all individuals who desired so-called occult knowledge have been regularly taken into the various Ray Temples or Retreats for training at night while the physical body lies sleeping. The Temples are open twenty-four hours a day round the globe so their facilities are always available to students. It should not be considered that this training is mystical: it is strictly utilitarian and practical and is designed to make physical plane living easier and more wholesome. It is designed to lead not to death, but to the Ascension for each individual.

For example, every great musical composer down through the ages has been a Temple student. Some composers are able to bring through their memories with greater accuracy than others. Wagner was an outstanding student in the Music Temple, and during his waking hours he was able to bring through musical notations with scarcely a deviation from the original Temple teachings. The story of Lohengrin is one of his finest examples.

It is presumed that Tesla not only had the usual free access to the Temples during his sleeping hours, but that he also had direct communication while in full waking consciousness. This is not unusual for even an advanced student; it is the normal practice for Initiates. In the outer world there is no information available on Tesla's exact evolutionary status on Venus, but it is known that the entire Venusian race is considered adept from our point of view. However, when space people take earth bodies they are often mercifully granted certain mental blockages for their own protection. That is, if a Venusian had a full and complete memory of his life on Venus, he would find it well nigh impossible to cope daily with earth situations. Even the Initiate Jesus did not have a complete mental grasp of His true mission until He was more than twelve years of age. It was then that He was taken to India for personal training under the supervision of His great teacher, the Christ, known in the outer world as Lord Maitreya.

John J. O'Neill has written a most detailed story of Tesla's life and scientific work in *Prodigal Genius*. But for those readers who are just becoming oriented in this field of study, it might be well to pause here for a brief review of the highlights that lighted the path of the man who came to earth to bring electricity to our homes and factories and illumination to our darkened minds.

Historians agree that Nikola Tesla was born at midnight, between July 9 and 10, in the year of 1856. Nikola himself hinted on a few occasions that this was not the date of his birth. These hints were disregarded along with hundreds of other statements made by Tesla, because in most quarters, he was regarded as being a bit impractical. This was not a criticism, for his genius was so highly respected that it was generally conceded that he did not have to measure up to conventional standards. He was to be allowed his little eccentricities, his passing fancies. The space people have now stated that Nikola was born on board their ship on a flight from Venus, and that they landed on the earth at midnight, between July 9 and 10, 1856.

When the space people say that Nikola was *born* on board one of their ships, they do not man that it was a physical birth. Physical conception and the birthing processes known on this planet are not used elsewhere. A sex system was introduced here after the laggards came, in order to keep the race in manifestation, and to provide for re-embodiment in groups bound by karma. This allowed karmic debts to be paid off in kind under the old law of "an eye for an eye, and a tooth for a tooth." On other planets positive and negative light rays are used to produce a physical form which can be occupied by an evolving lifestream. The form is of full stature. It is only on this planet that tiny, baby forms are utilized.

Djouka Tesla, the earth mother who cared for Nikola with a rare tenderness, was a most remarkable woman and assuredly possessed advanced spiritual powers. It has been said that she, too, was a Venusian, and if this is true, it accounts for her very unusual abilities. She was the eldest child in a family of seven children. Her father was a minister of the Serbian Orthodox Church. Her mother had become blind after the seventh child was born and Djouka unhesitatingly took charge of the entire household. She never attended school, nor did she learn even the rudiments of reading and writing at home. Yet she moved with ease in cultured circles, as did her family. Here was a woman who could neither read nor write, yet she possessed literary abilities far beyond those of a person of considerable education.

Tesla, himself, never wearied of talking about his remarkable mother, and described how she had absorbed "by ear" all the cultural riches of her community and her nation. Like Nikola, she apparently had the power of instant recall. Nikola said that she could easily recite, without error, long passages from the Bible; she could repeat thousands of versus of the national poetry of her country. It was because of her great interest in poetry that Nikola, in his busy American days as a superman, still found time to translate and have published some of the best examples of Serbian sagas.

His mother was also famed throughout her home provinces for her artistic ability, often expressed in beautiful needlework. She possessed remarkable manual dexterity, and Nikola said her fingers were so sensitive that she could tie three knots in an eyelash—even when she was past sixty years of age.

She had an excellent grasp of philosophy and apparently a practical understanding of mechanical and technical devices. She needed a loom for household weaving, so she designed and built one. She did not think of herself as an inventor, yet she built many labor-saving devices and instruments for her household. In addition she was so skillful in handling business and financial matters that she managed all accounts for her household as well as for her husband's church.

Nikola's earth father was the son of an army officer, and as a young man set out on a military career. But he was soon disillusioned for he was irked by the discipline, and turned to his true calling in the literary field. He wrote poetry, articles on current problems, and philosophical essays. This led, quite naturally, to the ministry, giving him an opportunity to write sermons and to speak from the pulpit. He did not limit himself to the usual church topics, but ranged far and wide, covering subjects of local and national interest concerning labor, social and economic problems. Until Nikola was seven years of age, the father had a parish church at Smiljan, an agricultural community in a high plateau region in that part of the Alps which stretch from Switzerland to Greece.

This then was the childhood environment of the boy from Venus. It was a life filled with joy. He had an ideal home with a loving understanding family. He lived in a magnificent countryside, close to nature. He was a boy like other little boys up to a certain point, the point at which he became the superboy, foreshadowing the superman. And so it was that he lacked human companions, a state not of loneliness but of aloneness, that was to continue throughout his physical incarnation. The unlighted ones whom he met everywhere through the years felt sorry for him because they assumed he was lonely. Tesla never tried to explain his position for he knew he would meet with no understanding from an alien world. To the end of his time in a physical body he lived at the very center, the very core, of a magnificent solitude, listening always to the Voice of the Silence.

As a boy Nikola liked nothing better than to wander the woods and over the mountains near his home. His little friends did not understand or share his boundless enthusiasm for trees, streams, birds and their nests, sunshine, clouds and stormy skies. Nor did they enjoy what they considered the hard work connected with Nikola's many boyhood inventions. He was constantly engaged in experiments that often failed, a fact which made them all the more fascinating. In reviewing his life in later years, he could look back upon these many lines of investigation which he had started as a boy and see how they led directly to some of his major inventions.

As he grew to maturity he displayed certain characteristics which might have revealed his Venusian origin had they been understood. His hands were unusually long, particularly his thumbs, and were extremely sensitive, carrying strong clean etheric currents. Inasmuch as he was clairvoyant he could easily see the murky gray astral matter which exudes from the hands of the ordinary person, an effluvia of filth so sticky that it will adhere to the etheric structure another person—even an individual occupying a body of high vibrations.

For this reason Tesla always dreaded shaking hands, tried to avoid such contacts even at the cost of being thought inconsiderate or impolite. On occasion, when it was absolutely necessary for him to shake hands with certain visitors in his New York office, he escaped at the earliest possible moment to his private washroom where he thoroughly washed his hands, drying them on a clean towel which was handed to him by his secretary and used only once.

He had the deep-set piercing eyes of the Initiate, clear blue in color. He also breathed correctly, something an earth person seldom achieves. This was a natural faculty, for as a small child he discovered that by breathing deeply he was overcome by a

feeling of lightness in his body. He felt so weightless that he concluded he would be able to fly if he developed the will to do so. It
is said that he did not know he was unusual in this respect while
he was still a child. Tesla could leave his body at will when he
grew older. He always lived in hotels, and his orders were that
he was never to be disturbed in his locked room. Tesla used pro-
jected consciousness as do all Initiates, although this is not to be
confused with the type of astral projection practiced by the average person. The Initiate uses many types of etheric energies
freely and in a manner which is always spiritually correct. The
ordinary individual does not have the ability to utilize these
energies or even to contact them, and therefore easily falls into
the dangerous practice of using astral or lower mental forces.
This leads to the next step on the left-hand path—the slate of
trance mediumship.

When Tesla was a small boy and found that his rhythmic
breathing gave him a feeling that he could fly, he quite naturally
and normally began to practice levitation. In this is a profound
lesson for all of us, and it is the same lesson that Jesus stressed.
Jesus warned us that we should not accept appearances, if those
appearances might prove limiting to us. We are always imitating
that which we see about us. We see people growing old, so we
grow old. If everyone thought of growing younger, and youth
began to manifest all about us, we would grow younger in
appearance as a matter of course. We see people walking, so we
walk. Young Nikola saw people walking, but he knew in his
heart that it was a cumbersome and laborious method, so he
pondered over it and got the *feeling* that he could fly. Then he followed his own inner feeling; not the example set by appearances
all about him. He rose from the earth, levitated, and moved
through space freely.

It might have startled unsuspecting New Yorkers to see
Tesla take off like his companion, the White Dove, and fly over
the city. But those who understand levitation and use it can also
throw a cloak of invisibility about themselves. People jumped to
strange conclusions about what they thought were the eccentricities of a great scientist. Another Great One by the name of
Jesus walked on water, and the curious are still talking about it

today. Tesla well knew that it was the better part of wisdom to remain invisible when he had his feet off the ground, so to speak.

Some of his close associates knew that he could levitate and respected the confidence. It might be well to underscore a point here—the person who levitates by using his Christ Principle to do so, must have a purpose behind his action, and it must be a purpose which is in some way furthering the Divine Plan. It is not spiritually permissible to levitate merely as a form of entertainment, for oneself or for others. Levitation is correctly used only if one is definitely going somewhere for a definite reason in the service of humanity. The average individual moves according to his own whim and pleasure, and usually to satisfy some personal objective which is often unnecessary. The average person moves about because of restlessness and an inherent inability to work according to any plan, let alone the Divine Plan.

The limitations of walking have offered certain advantages in the past. Transportation was so difficult that people tended to remain quiet as much as possible, or if they did go on a walking journey they often utilized the time to commune with nature or their fellowmen. But the advent of the automobile, bus, plane, and train, has introduced a method of transportation which adds only noise, confusion and chaos to the general picture, and which constantly exposes the emotional body to jarring impacts of a most distressing sort.

When Nikola was five years of age, he designed and installed a waterwheel across a mountain brook near his home at Smiljan. He utilized a disk cut from a tree trunk by lumber workers, some small branches, sticks and rocks. The device was a wonderful success from the standpoint of the young inventor. It was a bit crude, but it rotated. He had used the methods of antiquity in designing his model and it was only much later that he discovered that waterwheels have paddles, but his wheel operated without paddles.

This waterwheel was his first demonstration of a lesson he never forgot—to utilize free energy which was being constantly and freely replaced by Nature. Later, perhaps as a direct result of this experiment as a five-year-old boy, he developed the smooth-disk turbine. Later, too, he carried his experiments in utilizing the free energy of Nature into the atmosphere, and there he found that electricity in unlimited abundance would give him unlimited power—free energy that would carry mankind itself to freedom from the great curse of grueling labor. This was Tesla's magnificent concept that dominated his every thought as an inventor—free energy for a free world. It was the concept that carried him to the heights of cosmic fellowship, and the one mighty flame of inspiration which he set before his disciples as an eternal beacon—free energy to make and keep the people free.

When he was nine years old, he designed his first motor. It was made from tiny pieces of wood and shaped somewhat like a windmill. But it was not powered by the wind. It was powered by June bugs, flying round and round, trying to detach their feed from the glue which held them fast to their duties.

An incident took place at this time which clearly indicated the clean and wholesome trend of Tesla's thinking. He used June bugs because he needed to somehow capture power from the air although the bugs might have been happier had they not been drafted for this service. But Nikola used bugs just as a plowman would use horses. However, a little companion came in to observe the motor. He spied a reserve supply of June bugs which Nikola had placed in a small jar and the child grabbed a handful of the bugs and ate them. Nikola was so sickened by the event that he set the remaining bugs free and never again utilized bug-power. This was his first direct step toward capturing power from the air without enslavement of animal and human labor.

It was also at this time, when he was finishing his elementary studies and entering the Gymnasium for more advanced school work, that he first came to grips with his occult power of working in the fourth ether. He had only to think of an object, and it would appear before him, exhibiting the normal appearance of mass, solidity and dimensions. He had discussed this matter in confidence with his mother, for he found the ability to be a nuisance rather than an asset and wished to be rid of it.

Whether or not his mother could explain it was never revealed; now in retrospect it seems that she herself probably possessed the same power and understood it thoroughly. But Nikola was still a child and his mother agreed with him that he should attempt to banish the visions if he wished. From the occult point of view this was the correct thing to do, for no adult person should ever try to influence a child or tamper with a child's efforts to come to grips with spiritual realities. This kind of tampering has proved to be the great curse of churchianity and one of the most dangerous of black magic practices.

A little later Nikola confided to his mother that he wished to keep and use the power to envision objects before him, but that he wished to bring it under complete control. Again his mother agreed with him. The power to work in the fourth ether—a physical substance which forms the plane of density just a little finer than gas—is a power possessed in full by every advanced Initiate. They also work freely in the third, second and first ethers, which together with the lower four—physical, liquid, gaseous and the fourth ether-form the seven ethers which comprise the entire plane of matter. Scientists have not worked with the ethers because they could not see them, and it is not generally realized that the dense physical plane is only concretized ether. There is nothing mystical about working in the finer ethers; in fact, it is a scientific shortcut. There is actually no reason to dig gold out of the earth and then process it. It is much easier to extract it from the ether and precipitate it on to the physical plane. But in an earlier chapter of this book it was explained that after the laggards came man lost his power to precipitate matter, for he lost the use of the Rays. It was only then that man started digging in the soil and extracting his needs from the lowest plane of matter.

The powers possessed by Nikola Tesla were in no sense psychic powers. The ability to see into the fourth ether, to mold the etheric substance into machinery as did Tesla, and then to test that etheric machinery and make any necessary adjustments as did Tesla—all of this has nothing whatever to do with the astral plane. The astral plane is man-made. Astral matter is filthy matter. Tesla struck right through the astral plane and had no contact with it. As Arthur H. Matthews has truly stated: When Tesla wanted something he went straight to God.

The part which Nikola Tesla was to play in the Divine plan unfolded quickly when he enrolled at the gymnasium at Gospic, a large town to which his father had been assigned as a minister. He discovered that his favorite subject was mathematics. So intense was his devotion to this study that his teachers had to overlook his loathing for freehand drawing. It was thought that Nikola was unhappy about drawing because he was left-handed at that time. Eventually he became ambidextrous, another mark of the Initiate.

Many years later it was clearly demonstrated that Nikola loathed drawing because he could work in the fourth ether so easily, designing and building his machines in etheric substance, testing them and making necessary adjustments in the ether, and then leaving them "on file" in the ether. For him drawing was utterly unrealistic and an unmitigated nuisance. He did not have to make plans and jot down dimensions, because of his power of instant recall. After designing a machine in etheric substance he might have no occasion to think of it again for a period of five years or so. Yet when he did need the design he could call it up instantly before him, complete with exact dimensions.

In the school at Gospic, Nikola first came to desire to keep this power which he had possessed since birth, but he also desired to bring it under full control and use it, rather than allow it to use him and enslave him. Nikola had no wish to be submerged in paper work, even in his schooldays—a thought which might be of value to many business and government executives today.

Nikola found that he did not need to go to the blackboard in the classroom to work out a problem. At the thought of "blackboard" it appeared in the ether before him. As the problem was stated, it appeared instantly on the etheric blackboard, together with all the symbols and operations required to work out the solution. Each step appeared instantly, and much more rapidly than anyone could possibly work out the problem on paper or slate. Therefore, by the time the whole problem had been stated, Nikola could give the solution immediately.

At first his teachers thought he was just an extremely clever boy who had found some method of cheating. However, in a short time they were forced to admit that no deception could possibly be practiced, so they gladly accepted the glamour shed abroad as the rumor got around that the Gospic classroom was graced by a genius. Nikola never bothered to explain about the etheric blackboard for he intuitively knew that he would be casting pearls. Always through the passing years he guarded his power as the great spiritual treasure he knew it to be.

He used the same power to replace all customary memory functions, and he soon discovered that he could learn foreign languages with little of the usual effort. He became proficient in German, French and Italian in those early years, and this opened up to him entire new worlds that remained closed to other students. His father's library contained hundreds of fine books and by the time Nikola was eleven years old he had read them all. He had little in common with his schoolmates, and, in fact, little in common with his teachers. But they accepted him because he was a lovable lad without a trace of arrogance or pride. But neither did he shroud himself in an exaggerated sense of humility. He was a normal, natural friendly boy living in a natural, friendly world.

On fine summer days he would often wander over the mountains from Gospic to sit again beside the brook at Smiljin, and watch his little waterwheel in operation—the wheel he had designed and installed at the age of five years. He was constantly working on mechanical devices during the years he was in school at Gospic, but the school offered no courses that could help him—not even a course in manual training.

However, he did bring into focus one decision that foreshadowed the superman. The school on one occasion arranged an exhibit of models of waterwheels. They were not working models but Nikola could easily envision them in full action. In his home hung a picture which he had often carefully studied. His father explained that it was a picture of Niagara Falls in America.

In school, Nikola looked at the model waterwheels. At home he gazed again at the picture of Niagara Falls. Filled with prophetic joy he exultantly turned to his father and said: "Someday I am going to America and harness Niagara Falls for power." Thirty years later he carried out his plan, exactly as he had predicted it at the age of ten years.

Two other experiments which he worked on during these childhood years proved to be starting points for mature inventions. He discovered that air leaking into a vacuum produced a small amount of rotation in a cylinder. This was not the result he had intended, but he accepted it, and many, many years later, it led to his invention of the Tesla turbine, or what he called a "powerhouse in a hat" because it broke all records for horsepower developed per pound of weight.

The other experiment has not been carried out to its final conclusion, but now that Tesla has shed his physical body, he is working on it from the Inner Planes. In some form it will be presented as a New Age development under the general heading of weather control. While wandering in the mountains one day a thunderstorm broke overhead, and Nikola saw the lightning flash and then saw the rain come down in torrents. He reasoned that the lightning had produced the downpour.

Scientists, years later, argued that high up in the air the rain had come first, and the lightning followed. The raindrops fell slowly to earth, while the lightning flash was observed in a fraction of a second. But Tesla somehow knew that if he could produce lightning he could control the weather.

He never placed any limits on his thinking and even while walking over the mountains, through the downpour, he envisioned the day when rain could be produced when and where needed, thus providing an abundant food supply the world round. He never lost this vision, and thirty years later, in the mountains of Colorado, he produced bolts of lightning. He planned to use such bolts in his rain-making device, but was stopped by the United States Patent Office which refused to go along with his invention.

Now it can be readily seen that his invention might have been premature. For both rain and lightning are produced by the activities of the angelic kingdom. The water devas, fire devas and wind devas serve as housekeepers in the atmosphere around the planet. When they wish to wash out a certain section of the atmosphere, they produce as much rain as they need, and shoot bolts of lightning through the skies to counteract poisonous astral accumulations. The amount of rain that happens to fall on the ground depends entirely upon how much scrubbing is being done up yonder. When the scrub pails are emptied the rain stops.

The devas are not charged with duties such as going around with watering pots for the purpose of irrigating gardens. That problem is in the human province. The devas are very responsive and can be called into action by invocation; or when enough water has been sprinkled and floods threaten they can be stopped by invocation. Human beings should be trained to recognize their own karmic results and do something intelligent about it instead of moaning about the weather. All weather conditions can be under human control. Noah tackled that problem and took the steps necessary to deal with it. Then he sent forth the dove from the ark, and the dove returned with a plucked olive leaf, the symbol of peaceful waters subsiding from the flooded lands. But the dove cannot return unless people first send the dove forth.

When Tesla walked through the rainstorm he was witnessing angelic activities, even though he might not have thought of the matter in quite that way. But he knew that somehow his true work belonged up there in space, high above the mountains of earth. He knew that all worthwhile works must start at the Source. He knew that if he could understand the wonders of flashing lightning and streaming rain then weather could be mechanically controlled. He was correct, for while weather can be controlled through human invocation to the angels, it can also be controlled by a mechanical device. This will be another scientific revelation of the New Age; another proof that the old nonsensical concepts concerning mysticism must go, along with the old concepts about floods and droughts.

Nikola had distinguished himself as a scholar at the age of fourteen. That was in the year of 1870, and his schooldays at Gospic were over. He was a sensitive lad, highly intuitive, alert to the constancy of angels and the stupidities of men. His strength was actually extraordinary, for he often read and studied the whole night through, attended his classes by day, and completed a vast educational program of his own outside school hours. But because of his extreme sensitivity, his slim build, and his fastidious nature that demanded a degree of cleanliness far beyond the call of duty, his father felt that the boy was in delicate health.

His father was determined to protect him, and as it turned out the protective attitude paid dividends a few years later, when Nikola was spared compulsory military duty because his father was convinced that his delicate son would never survive army life. Nikola, in accord with his father's carefully planned arrangements, was forced to hide out in the mountains for more than a year while apparently attempting to recover his health. During this time his father was able to make certain contacts among the military, so that his son's absence was conveniently overlooked.

Nikola himself found military duty a subject so loathsome that he could not even bring himself to think about it. Intuitively he knew he would never serve in the army, so he made the most of his year of mountain solitude, and returned to his home in good health and with his head filled with scientific plans that, if carried out, probably would have proved earth-shaking in a most literal way.

But all this took place when he reached military age. His first serious difficulties started in 1870 when he finished school at Gospic. Because of his sensitive nature, his father felt that he should not continue his studies, but should go directly into the ministry. His scholarship at the age of fourteen was sufficiently outstanding to equip him to serve in the church.

So far as Nikola was concerned, the church was as bad as the army, and, in fact, worse, for the army was still some distance in the future but the church was at hand. Moreover, he had already decided on university training in electrical engineering, and was a dedicated disciple anxious to be about his Father's business in the cosmos. When an individual of the spiritual nature of Tesla comes into incarnation nothing is allowed to interfere with the purpose outlined on the Inner Planes. Plans for the embodiment are carefully arranged in accordance with the Divine Plan for the whole project under development. Initiates work with a high degree of spiritual efficiency. Certain universal needs are scheduled which must be met within time limits by certain disciples appointed to the task, and all of these plans must dovetail according to a certain predetermined pattern.

At this particular point Nikola had to be saved from a career in the church. The point could not be argued, especially between parents and a 14-year-old boy. Moreover, under Law the free will of the family members had to be permitted full sway; between the three of them they had to come to free will decision, but at the same time the decision had to be the correct one. Free will is somewhat paradoxical in any case, but especially so in the case of disciples. That is why discipleship is always fraught with extreme difficulty. The disciple is called upon to make a decision, and yet he must make the correct one which stands upon the Inner Planes and he must meet a time schedule. But happily a way is always provided, though it may be a way of severe struggle.

In the case of Nikola it was the way of psychic illness and was far from pleasant. He lapsed into a lethargic state from which he could scarcely be roused at times. His parents were frightened. The doctors admitted they were helpless as they had no idea what was causing the illness. When it reached a critical stage they simply gave up all hope of saving his life.

Naturally the doctors in Gospic had no idea whatever about the true nature of Nikola's illness. Even medical science today knows nothing of "soul sickness" or the diseases which attack only disciples and not the average person. The individual himself, however, is usually able to supply the answer for he is under guidance from the Inner Planes. So after the Gospic doctors had given up hope for his life, and his parents had become somewhat resigned, Nikola turned to his books. He had been working in the local library at Gospic and had carried home an armful of selections just before his illness.

Listlessly he looked them over. He found one by Mark Twain. In it he suddenly discovered a paragraph which brought instant illumination. His enthusiasm for life was rekindled. The crisis passed. His health returned to normal. Nikola himself understood with profound conviction that it was the writings of

67

Mark Twain that had saved his life. He never forgot the incident to the end of his days, and often spoke of his heartfelt gratitude to Mark Twain. Many years after the Gospic incident the two men met in New York and became very close friends. When Tesla himself had only a short time left on earth, and Mark Twain had been gone from the mortal scene for years, Tesla spoke of Mark coming to see him in his hotel room, and of their having a long visit together. When Tesla was reminded that Mark Twain had been dead for years, he vigorously denied it, adding that he was very much alive.

As indeed he is, even though invisible to certain people—the very same sort of people who fail to see through the humorous philosophy of Mark Twain, and into the supernal light beyond. What did Mark and Nikola talk about in that memorable conversation which took place on a January day in 1943, in a New York hotel room, where Tesla's physical body lay breathing lightly in almost final readiness for departure?

Mark and Nikola were old friends, companions of ancient days in starry space. Like all such gentle humorists, like all such compassionate observers of human folly, like all old friends, they met on that occasion of joyous reunion, and they talked about the weather.

Standing there together in their magnificent clean bogies of vibrant light, it was only natural that their conversation should turn to that earlier sickroom scene in Gospic, when Nikola, with the vital help of high-frequency energies pouring from Mark's written words, had firmly set his course once again into an uncertain future among foolish mortals. It was Mark who had glimpsed the mortals in a humorous moment, when they had reached an ebb point in their foolishness—a point where everybody talked about the weather, but nobody did anything about it.

That vibrant instant with Mark had set Nikola free from his illness in Gospic. Nobody did anything about the weather, Mark said. But Nikola joyfully remembered that he had determined to do something about it years earlier when he walked through a mountain thunderstorm. He was going to learn to control lightning, and thereby control the weather. He was the Somebody whose inventions would liberate and illumine all the negative nobodies of the world.

Yes, that was what they talked about, the author and the inventor, on a day in January, 1943.

The Gospic illness over, Nikola was ready to be guided to his next necessary advancement. His father had been thoroughly frightened and was now anxious to humor the boy by permitting him to go to college at Carlstadt in Croatia. Upon arriving in that city, Nikola took up residence with relatives, but his years in their home were unhappy ones. Almost at once he contracted malaria, but he insisted upon starting his classes at the college.

His brilliance undimmed by either illness or lack of family harmony, he completed the four-year college course in three years. He carried away with him one lasting impression which was to make everything easier in his life thereafter. His professor of physics had held him enthralled with demonstrations of feats performed with laboratory apparatus. Tesla knew beyond a shadow of a doubt that his life was to be fully and completely dedicated to a study of electricity.

With his life stretching complete before him, he returned home, only to face up to the demands of the army. Again he suddenly fell into a psychic illness. Again doctors gave up all hope of saving his life. A cholera epidemic raged in the town, and it was presumed that he had cholera in addition to malaria, plus the nervous strain brought on by his college work, plus undernourishment resulting from the unhappy culinary situation in the home of his relatives in Carlstadt.

However, from the occult point of view Nikola suffered from a psychic illness in order to prevent a greater tragedy—compulsory military service. During the long illness which steadily became worse, Nikola's father became more and more frightened. The space people have not explained how much Nikola's father knew about the boy's origin. Of course, his mother had to know the details, but it is fairly clear that she herself was originally a Venusian. Perhaps the father was not, and it is even possible that Nikola was placed in the care of the mother without the father knowing of his origin: this all happened long ago in a remote mountain province. Women gave birth to children, often alone, or with only a midwife or neighbor in attendance. There are many possible explanations.

At any rate, whatever his understanding about his son, the Rev. Milutin Tesla was ready to accept anything to save the life of Nikola at a moment when the boy was drifting off into unconsciousness, from which it seemed apparent he would not emerge. His father, in a firm, clear voice, commanded him not to die. In exchange, Nikola used his few remaining breaths to gasp out the news that he would remain if his father would let him become an electrical engineer. The bargain was struck on the instant, and within a matter of seconds vital energy began pouring through the tired body. In a few days Nikola was up and about and life was glorious once more.

The shadow of death had hovered close and then withdrawn. The shadow of the army loomed directly ahead. But Nikola's father had given his promise. Nikola was to be an electrical engineer and the army was to be minus one recruit. It was then that Nikola's father realized that his son needed at least a year's vacation in the mountains in order to regain not only his health but his freedom. Hurriedly, Nikola was provided with a hunting outfit, some books and papers. He was gone before anyone in Gospic knew he had risen from his deathbed.

In 1873 Nikola went to Gratz to study electrical engineering. He knew that the forces of destiny were shaping him for a great purpose, and during his first year at Gratz he did more than twice the amount of work required, passing all examinations with the highest marks that could be awarded. He hoped in this way to express his appreciation to his parents for saving him from army service and for permitting him to study electrical engineering, but because they feared he was again undermining his health they did not receive the news of his high marks with joy.

During the second year he limited his studies to physics, mathematics and mechanics in order to placate his parents. Actually, however, he was guided in this decision by higher forces, for it was important that he have plenty of leisure time to devote to the next step in his unfoldment.

A piece of electrical equipment, a Gramme machine, that

could be used as either a dynamo or motor, had been acquired by the Institute. It was a direct-current machine, and was demonstrated to the class. It did not please Tesla, because a great deal of sparking took place at the commutator.

The professor explained that as long as electricity flowed in one direction, a commutator would be necessary to change the direction, and the sparking could, therefore, not be avoided. Tesla replied that by using alternating current the commutator could be eliminated.

The professor was waiting for this suggestion and let loose a storm of criticism. He informed Tesla, in an abrupt and lofty professorial manner, that many men had already experimented with alternating current, and it was simply not feasible. In that instant, Tesla had an intuitive flash. He knew the professor was wrong; he knew alternating current was possible; he knew that he would and could demonstrate it. The argument between the student and teacher went on during the remainder of the term, and although Tesla was unable to bring his vision down to practical results, he was by no means discouraged. The professor stated that Tesla's theories were contradicted by Nature and that settled the matter. It was far from settled in Tesla's mind.

The following year Tesla was to go to the University of Prague, but a lucrative position was offered him, so he saved his earnings, and enrolled at the university a year later. He extended his studies in physics and mathematics, but the vision of alternating current remained ever before him. In his heart he knew that he would make the great discovery that would elevate the infant science of electricity to the maturity of a great power.

Just after his graduation from the University of Prague his father died, and then Tesla set about to become self-supporting. The telephone invented by Alexander Graham Bell was making its advent in Europe at this time and in 1881, he was placed in charge of the new telephone exchange in Budapest. While there he developed an amplifier, which led to the present amplifiers on radio sets. He never patented the device, however, as his sole interest was still the problem of alternating current.

At this time, he underwent another severe psychic illness, during which his sense organs were affected by acute sensitivity.

71

Apparently his vibrations were raised for some occult reason, and although doctors despaired of saving his life, he came through the period of suffering and his vibrations were restored to normal. But during the illness his dedication to the problem of alternating current had fully crystallized. He could scarcely think of anything else, and he knew that if he stopped working on it he would die, if he failed; he would likewise perish.

He was a man without a choice, and on a late afternoon in February, 1882, he had recovered sufficiently to take a walk in a park in Budapest. His companion was a former classmate by the name of Szigeti. The two young men walked toward the setting sun. The skies ahead were painted with colors of high brilliance. Tesla was reciting aloud Goethe's *Faust*. It was a cosmic moment and Tesla was at one with the angels. Suddenly he stopped in a rigid pose. "Watch me," he cried out. "Watch me reverse it."

His startled companion was thrown into a state of panic, for Tesla seemed to be gazing at the sunset, and Szigeti feared that Tesla thought he could reverse the sun.

Szigeti suggested that they rest a moment, but Tesla talked on excitedly, looking steadily at something directly in front of him. Szigeti could see nothing, but Tesla was calling out in an exultant voice: "See how smoothly it runs. Now watch me stop it. Then start it. It goes just as smoothly in the opposite direction!"

Eventually Tesla became somewhat more composed and explained to his companion that he had just solved the problem of alternating current. He also revealed to Szigeti that he could see the motor before him, in full operation, and that he would not need to make drawings. But for the benefit of his friend who could see nothing but clear air in the spot where Tesla was operating his motor, they returned home together and talked far into the hours of the night, discussing every detail of the discovery.

Shortly thereafter Tesla was recommended for a job in Paris, and he was pleased to go to that city because it meant many contacts with Americans, who were interested in all sorts of mechanical developments. Meanwhile he had mentally built a complete alternating-current system, both two-phase and three or more. His famous polybase power system was a reality. As usual, he designed his dynamos, motors, transformers, and all other devices in the fourth ether, performing his mathematical calculations on the etheric "blackboard" just as in his school-days. He could test these mental constructs by leaving the machines in the ether to run for weeks. He would then examine them for signs of wear.

When he arrived in Paris he formulated a certain living pattern to which he adhered for the rest of his life, insofar as possible, or insofar as money would permit. He was always meticulously neat in dress, full of self-confidence, and carried himself with a poised, quiet attitude. For many years he had never rested more than five hours at night, and he claimed that he never slept more than two hours out of the five.

In Paris he would rise at five, swim in the Seine for half an hour, then dress and walk briskly for more than an hour to his place of work. He then ate a hearty breakfast, and by half-past eight he was ready for his duties. In the evening he would return to the center of Paris, dine at the best cafes, and contact any companions who were willing to listen to him describe his polyphase alternating current system.

At this point Tesla demonstrated that he was a world dis-ciple, pledged to serve humanity and not a privileged group, for he never developed a secretive attitude about his inventions. He would gladly talk to anyone who would listen. He wanted only one thing—to give his invention to the human race so that all might benefit from it. He knew there was a fortune in it, but he was never concerned about the process of extracting fortunes from his machines.

He did not understand anything about money-making. This was due to the fact that he was a Venusian, and had not had any previous training in handling money. Money as we know it does not exist on Venus or anywhere in this solar system. The solar system operates on a basis of spiritual economy in which God's unlimited abundance and supply is accepted as Divine Law. A man-made money system such as exists on this planet is a direct contradiction of that law. Further, the money system was cre-ated here as an instrument to serve the forces of darkness and has been used for the enslavement of humanity. Paul knew exactly what he was talking about when he stated that love of money was the root of all evil.

Tesla may have known nothing about money-making in the commercial shopping sense, but he had a deep understanding of the evils of the money system on this planet. In fact, his understanding in this regard was so profound that he never made the slightest attempt to come to terms with banking interests, because he realized that in doing so he would be coming to terms with the dark forces themselves. However, he was not going to take time out from his work to attempt to explain his attitude to anyone, so he just went ahead with his job of serving humanity and the Forces of Light, and left others to serve the devil if they wished. Tesla was not a reformer. He was a transformer. His job was to transform the world from darkness to light, from enslavement to freedom.

Tesla made every effort to break down any secrecy surrounding his inventions. He was ready and willing to explain to all who would listen. There was no danger of his inventions being stolen at that time. In fact he could not even give them away. The forces of darkness were already securely entrenched in the electrical field. They wanted no part of any invention designed by a White Magician. Well they knew that if Tesla ever invaded the electrical field in global fashion it would mark the end of the old way of life with all its international complexities— its evil money system, its corrupt political delusions, its churchianity, its educational inadequacies.

There remained nearly twenty years until the turn of the century, and yet Tesla stood as the great colossus, the mighty genius who, working hand-in-hand with his Creator, might have saved the world from further violence of clashing forces of evil. Years later, when alternating current was finally adopted in America through the good offices of George Westinghouse, the dark forces still fought to turn the tide against Tesla. Finally they capitulated and took the opposite stand. They supported the adoption of alternating current and its widespread use, but only when they found that Tesla had outwitted them by obsoleting his own invention. He abandoned the whole system set up around the distribution of electricity by wires and developed a World Wireless System whereby everyone could have all the electricity they wished by merely attaching a small antenna to home, shop or office building.

The forces of darkness would have none of this and to this day, they have been successful in preventing the wireless system from reaching the attention of the public which would demand its use. But now Tesla, working in the scientific department of Shamballa, has again had the last Word to say through his disciple, Otis T. Carr of Baltimore. As the New Age advances it is quite likely that Tesla's wireless system for electrical distribution may be obsoleted by Carr's free-energy devices. And so it is that the Legions of Light move steadily on to Victory.

As the new civilization takes shape it will be clearly seen that Tesla had access to no secrets at any time. He had direct contact with Universal Truth. Tesla worked out ways and means to anchor Truth on the physical plane through using physical matter. The early Root Races on the planet worked in exactly the same manner. They brought down and anchored in physical matter the higher vibrations direct from the Godhead. Matter is spirit slowed down; spirit is matter speeded up. All is One.

The anchoring of Truth, or the lowering of vibrations, has never been a secret process. It has always been part of the teachings of the Ageless Wisdom. But it is a well-known fact that you can't get Truth out of a man if he has no available Truth in him. Truth is Light. Light which is imprisoned or obscured cannot illumine a person. Only the individual with a clean atomic structure, or one who understands and practices transmutation, can hope to anchor Truth in physical matter. The average scientists, especially those contaminated by working with military weapons, are in no position to embark on a search for Truth. It will not be found in an H-bomb.

When Tesla agreed to undertake the task of bringing light to the earth he envisioned this globe as one vast terrestrial lamp spiralling toward its God-ordained destiny of perfected evolution; bearing upon its lighted body a race of Illumined Initiates, who have been freed from the cycle of rebirth, and are journeying back to their Source, to their appointed mansion in the Father's House.

This was Tesla's great secret, if secret he had. Let those who feel overlooked because they were not called upon to share it, ask themselves at this point if they are sure they are quite ready, even now, to share it. Or are they like those disciples of Jesus who had to listen to the Master tell them they were not ready to share the knowledge of certain things; that to speak of such Truths would place upon them a greater burden of Light than they could bear.

Tesla's life in Paris went on smoothly. He enjoyed robust health. But he was employed by the Continental Edison Company, working all day on direct-current machines, and this proved to be an irksome point. His superior alternating-current inventions, although still in the fourth ether, were tauntingly close at hand.

Finally, the situation was changed abruptly by an accident in the railway station at Strasburg in Alsace, where an Edison powerhouse and electric lights had been installed. Alsace then belonged to Germany and the electrical installation was formally opened with Kaiser William I present. Unfortunately, when the lights were turned on the glory was indeed brief, for a short circuit caused an entire wall of the railway station to be blown to bits.

Tesla was sent from Paris to Strasburg to survey the damage and proceed with repairs. Once the work got under way and he could serve in a supervisory capacity, he arranged for space and tools in a nearby machine shop, and there he proceeded to transfer his dream of alternating current from the fourth ether to the physical plane.

He was an amateur machinist but a meticulous worker, and gradually a large collection of miscellaneous parts of a two-phase alternating-current motor took shape in the machine shop. Tesla not only made each part exact to a thousandth of an inch, but he carefully polished it to make it more exact. He had no working drawings or blueprints. He formed each part from metal to exactly match the etheric part which he saw before him.

He did not have to test the parts because he knew they would fit. When he had finished the entire collection he quickly assembled the machine and started up his power generator. The cosmic moment had struck. He closed the switch. The armature of his motor turned, built up speed. He closed the reversing switch. The armature stood still, then instantly started turning in the opposite direction.

Alternating current had been transferred from the invisible to the visible, from the fourth ether to the dense physical plane, from a substance lighter than gas to metal.

So there in the noisy machine shop in Strasburg stood the very motor which Tesla had first discovered in the sunset glow in the park at Budapest, walking with his friend, Szigeti. Even the beautiful lines from Goethe's *Faust,* which he had been proclaiming aloud as he walked, were still appropriate:

"The glow retreats, done is the day of toil;

"It yonder bastes, new fields of life exploring;

"Ah, that no wing can lift me from the soil.

"Upon its track to follow, follow soaring...."

Tesla's unique method of constructing his first motor gives an excellent clue to the manner in which all Initiates consciously work, although they usually precipitate the etheric form instantly into physical matter, without intermediary construction work. They can externalize whatever they need by first visualizing it in the ethers, then calling it forth into physical density.

That is why spaceships are described as being constructed without rivets, welding, seams, or cracks around doors. They are not constructed but precipitated direct from the ether.

Since the laggards came and human beings forgot how to precipitate what they need, all man-made forms are first created in mental matter by a designer thinking through his problem and creating a thought-form. Mental matter is on the same plane as gas, and is, therefore, one density lower than the fourth ether. But mental matter is all that the average person can manipulate, and is not by any means pure, but is heavily weighted with astral accumulations. It is virtually impossible for the average person to create a clear, precise thoughtform, free from personal emotional distortions. Since he cannot control his mental constructs with any degree of success, his matrix or thoughtform is often composed more of fantasy than of fact. When it is lowered into form the physical plane result is often useless, ugly, and a spiritual monstrosity.

In the summer of 1884, shortly after Tesla returned from Strasburg to Paris, he arrived in New York City with exactly four cents in his pocket, and a book of his poems. In addition, he had a letter of introduction to Thomas A. Edison.

In a few brief weeks in Europe many things had happened to force this hurried and unplanned voyage to America. While Tesla was still in Strasburg he tried to interest business men there in his new alternating-current motor which he had built from the parts he had made by hand. He could not stir up a spark of enthusiasm for the machine which was later to revolutionize the electrical industry of the world. Then, when he returned to Paris to collect the substantial fee which he had been promised for getting the Strasburg installation in operation, the company conveniently failed to remember anything about the arrangement. One official, however, did suggest to Tesla that he go direct to Mr. Edison in America.

Within a few days Tesla sold his personal belongings, packed his bags, and bought his railroad and steamship tickets. However, just as he was about to board the train to take him from Paris to the ship he discovered he had been robbed. He ran along the moving train and boarded it, paying his fare with loose change and notes he had in his pockets after his wallet was stolen. He also boarded the ship, explaining that his ticket had been stolen. Fortunately, no one showed up to claim his reservations, so he was allowed to continue on his way to the United States. Without luggage and with only a few cents in change, he finally landed in New York.

He lacked fare for either cab or trolley, so he set out to walk from the pier to the home of a friend, for he had fortunately retained his address book. He walked past an electrical repair shop and inside he saw a weary and obviously harassed workman struggling to repair a machine.

He entered the shop. "Let me repair it," he said to the mechanic. The workman, without further ado, permitted Tesla to set to work. Although the task was difficult, Tesla finally had the machine operating. The grateful mechanic handed him twenty dollars and offered him a steady job. But Tesla thanked him, explaining that he was on his way to another job, and could not accept his.

He continued on his way, found his friend, and remained at his home overnight. The next morning he set out to call on Dr. Edison, who then had headquarters in New York on South Fifth Avenue, a street which later became known as West Broadway.

The meeting between the two men was not auspicious. Edison belonged to the direct-current school of thought, and Tesla was not only in opposition to direct current. but was actually the inventor of alternating current. Furthermore, Edison was lacking in technical education. He was totally unable to understand Tesla's ability to visualize a problem in its entirety without doing any mechanical work on it or following the usual trial-and-error method.

Yet Edison was conscious of Tesla's great value, and while he could not afford to hire him—he was a competitor advocating the direct-current method—yet he could not afford to let it be known that he had not hired him. Rather grudgingly he employed Tesla, and almost at once Edison was placed in a position from which only the incomparable Tesla could rescue him.

The finest passenger ship of the day was called the *Oregon*. Edison had installed one of his electric light plants on the steamship, and the vessel was ready to set sail. However, the lighting plant failed completely, and Edison was unable to find the cause of the difficulty. Tesla was dispatched to the ship late one afternoon and by the following morning had the dynamos functioning properly.

This incident served to advance his prestige with Edison. When he later approached Edison with a plan to improve the design of the Edison dynamos and at the same time lower the operating cost, Edison not only agreed, but offered Tesla a fee of $50,000 if the work came up to expectations.

Tesla labored at the task for many months, putting in many hours of overtime daily. He completed designs for twenty-four types of dynamos.

Some of the machines were built and tested and proved to be very satisfactory. Patents were taken out by Edison. When the entire job was finished. Tesla requested the $50,000 which he had been promised. Edison, however. claimed that the agreement had been merely a "joke," whereupon Tesla resigned his job immediately. The Strasburg incident had been repeated.

It was the year of 1885. Had Tesla known the heartaches that lay ahead he might not have had the courage to continue his efforts to provide alternating current for a world that seemed to offer him nothing but scorn. Looking back over Tesla's entire life, it can be seen that he never capitulated to the evil money system which prevails on this planet. Again and again, just as he was about to grasp and use the contaminated medium of exchange, it was snatched from him. This left Tesla free, but the karma engendered descended upon humanity.

Even today, years after Tesla's death, humanity still awaits the superman's great inventions which could give untold comfort to physical plane existence. And the reason?—a lack of adequate funds to develop the inventions on a world-wide scale. Tesla would settle for nothing short of global operations, bringing help to all the peoples of the earth. It is very significant that he wished to encompass the planet with his work, and in the case of the interplanetary communications set, the solar system. Being a Venusian he could not produce inventions that would remain earthbound. The superman was restless to grasp the extended hand of interplanetary friendship; to prepare the Dark Star of earth for its great cosmic initiation into solar freedom.

But in 1885, the financial world was not ready to give up its evil interests in the Dark Star. It perhaps is even less ready today, but today the Christ Forces have all dark manipulators on the run, and happily for humanity, it will be the last run. The Forces of Light are now able to stand firmly on the side of humanity and fight evil to the finish.

In 1885, financial matters were handled with shrewdness and cunning. Honesty was easily set aside by the fortunemakers of the day. At this time a group of promoters offered to finance a small company to promote Tesla. They were to pay him a modest salary and were to reward him on a grand scale with stock in the company. He thought he saw an opportunity to develop alternating current, but once the company had been formed, Tesla was obliged to develop an arc light for street and factory illumination.

It was to be a type of light which the promoters could use to further certain schemes of expansion.

The light was developed and Tesla took out patents of his design. However, the company had been organized in such a tricky manner that when Tesla was awarded his stock he soon found it to be worthless. The promoters prospered and Tesla was left without funds.

He then struck bottom in his American venture, for by the year of 1887, he was actually forced to dig ditches and take other laboring jobs at $2 a day. But even this provided the ladder on which he climbed to success, for the foreman in charge of the ditch digging recognized Tesla as a man of genius. He introduced him to Mr. A.K. Brown of the Western Union Telegraph Company. Mr. Brown, in turn, interested a friend in Tesla. The two men put up sufficient money to finance the Tesla Electric Company.

In April of 1887, Tesla opened his own laboratory and workshop on South Fifth Avenue, now West Broadway, and he found himself a neighbor of Edison. Edison had turned down Tesla's idea for alternating current, striving to boost the prestige of direct current. Yet, in the end, Tesla won the competitive fight, despite the fact that he was backed by limited funds while Edison was financed by J.P. Morgan.

Tesla's hour had struck and ever thereafter the Dark Star was to be illumined by his incomparable genius.

It is impossible, even today, to evaluate the virgin field of electrical science which Tesla explored within a few months after his new laboratory was opened. The United States Patent Office could not easily grasp the scope of his work. They considered his inventions so original and so basic that they simply started issuing a succession of patents that brought the new age of power to birth in one mighty surge of advancement.

The entire electrical world of 1887 was engulfed by the sweeping new advance. It can now be seen in retrospect that in the years which have since elapsed, civilization has not yet absorbed even the basic fundamental scientific achievements produced by Tesla. As for the philosophy of Tesla, it is hardly known that he had anything to offer in that field, as perhaps he did not—for his philosophy had already been presented by Jesus. Since western minds had failed to grasp even the basic teachings offered down through the countless centuries by the Hierarchy, and then had ignored the true meanings underlying the work of Jesus, it is abundantly clear why Tesla did not bother to waste his time tossing pearls.

Within six months after Tesla opened his laboratory in 1887, he applied to the Patent Office for a single patent covering his entire electrical system which he had designed at that time. The Patent Office was overwhelmed by this "package deal" and insisted that Tesla break his single patent down into seven parts. This was done, and in April of 1888, he applied for five more patents which were granted. Toward the end of 1888, he was issued eighteen additional patents.

By this time the entire scientific world was not only amazed, but completely baffled by the sudden manner in which their cherished concepts were swept away over night. It was not easy to make such a quick and monumental adjustment to new values, especially in view of the fact that many of the scientists and technicians of the day, then as now, prided themselves on being strong-minded, free-thinking men, who were capable of standing on their two feet and meeting the issues of the day.

They also prided themselves on being God-fearing men, independent men, who, if they wished to invent a machine, could do so without calling upon the aid of the Creator. But in some mysterious fashion the Creator had somehow got back on the job through Tesla. So these God-fearing men looked everywhere for the answer except in the right place. For a man who fears God can never love Him, and a man who places God on a pedestal high in the sky is most certainly in fear of Him. The only way to love God is to bring His energy down into dense matter by lowering the vibration, and then anchor it there. The early Root Races had the answer as did Tesla.

The social gossips of the day, back in 1888, also had their word to say about Tesla. To them he was at once the most fascinating and the most aggravating of men. He did not share their interests, and they could not seem to find a way of sharing his. It was incomprehensible to them that a man of such cosmopolitan tastes could overlook them so completely, so utterly. So far as women were concerned, Tesla was considered to be the world's most eligible bachelor. Ambitious mothers and anxious daughters hovered close, or at least let us say they tried. But no one ever got close to Tesla. So far as men were concerned, Tesla was constantly inventing machines which could be manufactured and sold. This stamped the sign of the dollar indelibly upon him. Over the years the Tesla-marriage-money subject became a topic of international conversation.

The next momentous Tesla development came on May 16, 1888, when, in response to an invitation, he gave a lecture and demonstration before the American Institute of Electrical Engineers. This lecture served notice upon the entire world that the greatest genius of the age had brought his discoveries to fruition, presenting civilization with alternating current, and thus setting electricity geographically free. Under Edison's direct current system it was necessary to have a powerhouse in the center of every square mile, or even closer in large cities. This presented an impossible situation if electricity was to become the planetary source of power that Tesla visualized.

Tesla had no desire to develop his inventions commercially, for he preferred to spend his time in research. He knew that the very inventions which he was in the process of patenting would become obsolete in a short time if he could continue his research. Edison fought resolutely to maintain the prestige of direct current, for he had invented the incandescent electric lamp, and in order to sell the lamps he had to make electricity available so that the lamps could be used. Moreover, Edison's financial interests were tied completely to those of J. P. Morgan, and Edison was not free to pursue any course except the strictly commercial one.

When Tesla gave his' famous lecture on May 16, 1888, George Westinghouse of Pittsburgh was in the audience. Westinghouse was already well known as the inventor of an air brake for trains and of many other electrical devices. He had made a fortune in exploiting his own inventions, and was a man of tremendous vision. He immediately recognized the vast possibilities, commercially and geographically, of Tesla's alternating current system. Shortly thereafter he contacted Tesla for an interview. In a matter of minutes Westinghouse agreed to pay Tesla one million dollars outright for the alternating current patents, plus a royalty of one dollar per horsepower.

It was Westinghouse, therefore, who seized the opportunity to develop Tesla's patents which would supply electricity to the entire world. In the few moments required to negotiate the deal, a friendship was formed between the two men which, in its magnificence and trust, was of transcendent beauty. As things worked out, the friendship was almost the only happy development that resulted from the meeting, but as the years passed Tesla never betrayed the slightest bitterness or regret over misfortunes that came to both of them as a result of their cooperation.

Tesla spent a useless, weary year in Pittsburgh attempting to get Westinghouse launched in his manufacturing efforts, but finally refused to remain longer. The Westinghouse engineers, accustomed to their own way of doing things, were baffled and confused by Tesla's magic. Tesla in turn had no way of communicating with the men since he could not get down to their level of understanding. Tesla was a great teacher of philosophy to certain individuals. He was also a great teacher of what might be called cosmic engineering—again to certain individuals. But he selected these individuals personally. They were disciples, but they were already active disciples for the Forces of Light.

To expect Tesla to go into a manufacturing plant and teach a group of American engineers at all stages of evolutionary development was, of course, ridiculous. But perhaps even Tesla did not realize the scope of his own greatness, and the intellectual gap which existed as a barrier between him and those of earth who had not yet attained discipleship. At any rate, after his departure from the Pittsburgh plant, the Westinghouse engineers worked out their own problems, and eventually the manufacturing process got under way.

Tesla returned to his own laboratory in New York, to his beloved research—a wealthy man, free from the need for commercialism. This freedom was for him the greatest triumph that might come to a human soul. Working again on research for his polyphase power system, he was granted forty-five patents in this country during the next four years, in addition to more than a hundred in foreign countries.

Edison had long been busy aiming competitive lances in all directions. He was strictly a commercial money-making man. He was untrained in the science of electrical engineering and, therefore, had to depend upon those whose services he could get for hire. He was tied, hand and foot, to the value of the dollar and was thereby forced into the role of a huckster. He could never shake himself free from the clutches of the monkey on his back in the form of the J.P. Morgan interests, although there is no evidence to show that he desired to do so. Some men are destined to play the role of the organ-grinder. It does not lie within the karmic patterns of all men to compose great music.

Edison had tangled with Westinghouse on many occasions. But when it was discovered that Westinghouse, capable and far-visioned, a successful inventor and a successful business man, had taken on the task of developing Tesla's alternating current, the battle took on a new and fiercer phase. It was at this time that the New York State Prison authorities stepped openly into the White Magic field of electricity, and turned it into the a field of black magic almost overnight. They adopted alternating current as developed by Tesla for the electrocution of condemned prisons.

Tesla claimed that the Edison interests had engineered the project to discredit alternating current. There was more than a little truth in this, as that was probably the original purpose. For the Edison interests, anxious to make a dollar even one jump ahead of the undertaker, had tried to provide direct current to power the electric chair. But they had failed, because the plain fact of the matter was that direct current could not be produced at the high voltages required. All this was lost on the public, however, as the Edison interests proclaimed from the housetops that the prison's choice of current was proof of the deadly danger of Tesla's invention.

Now we can look back and realize that this victory of the forces of darkness, operating from the astral plane directly through the prison authorities, touched off a retrogressive movement which has since carried certain aspects of civilization back to evil days which have not been known on this planet since the sinking of Atlantis.

Now people like to look back to the pre-atomic age, and blame the nuclear scientists for the present destructive threat to humanity. But nuclear scientists would not have had a ghost of a chance of exercising their black magic, had not the road to darkness been well paved already by black magicians long in control on the astral plane. The New York State prison authorities cooperated to the hilt in assisting the black magicians to take over control of the alternating-current invention and all humanity has suffered, by being robbed, and robbed, and robbed of the true advantages of the invention since that dreadful day.

The control by black magicians and their tools has since been broken on the Inner Planes, and even the tools will soon be eliminated from the physical plane. The Christ Forces, assisted by the angelic kingdom, have seized—and removed all black magicians from the planet. Their human tools still exist on the physical plane, by the thousands, but their nefarious endeavors will be smashed down as soon as the seventh Ray has done a bit more of its beneficent work of transmutation.

While New York State prison authorities were busying themselves in an all-out effort to lower the planetary vibrations by using electricity, the Third Aspect of God, or the Holy Spirit, to electrocute condemned prisoners, George Westinghouse prepared to use the Tesla invention of alternating current to put the entire United States on an electrical power basis. Tesla, meanwhile, back at his research, set about to make obsolete his earlier inventions, and place the entire world on one simple electrical system which would enable all of God's children, from the Arctic to the Antarctic, to have light—more abundant light and living advantages.

The year had turned to 1891. Tesla and Westinghouse were firmly aligned with the Divine Plan and their combined energies were enabling a tiny portion of this Plan to manifest. But where there is Light-in-Action on this Dark Star, it is always Consuming darkness. In other words, there has not yet come a time when we could say that we had a safe dividend of light left over for intelligent, constructive uses. Every unit of light released by disciples on this planet must still be used to illumine the suffering atoms wherein evil is bottled up in the form of astral debris.

In 1891, the karma that was being engendered by the New York State prison authorities alone, was so dense in its accumulation that the forces of darkness were enabled to sweep into the alternating-current field without hindrance. The black leaders were reinforced by a vast horde of disembodied criminals from the astral plane, bent on vengeance. They struck savagely at Westinghouse, for his company alone would supply the nation with alternating current, providing great wealth to Tesla for years to come in the form of royalties.

The dense overshadowing of the Westinghouse financial advisors commenced. In those days little was known about astral influences, and when the deluded, bewitched money men went into a panic, they merely thought they were being astute financial wizards. Here was a picture of little bigshots, utterly dazzled by the mocking brilliance of their own arrogance.

A number of quick mergers with smaller companies took place and a new unit was formed, known as the Westinghouse Electric and Manufacturing Company. But before this deal was finalized, the financial group put George Westinghouse on the spot, and told him that he was to destroy his contract with Tesla. The alternative? The money-men would destroy the Westinghouse organization as it existed at that time.

The financial wizards were crazed by their astral overshadowing, and goaded into a greedy desire to consume all. They were adamant in their determination to share no profits with anyone—not even with the goose Tesla, who had laid the golden egg. Against this mighty army of darkness, George Westinghouse stood out like a giant pillar of light—but a lone giant. The financial interests were set to see the company destroyed rather than yield a single dollar in royalties to Tesla.

But even one on the side of the Forces of Light is in itself a victorious majority against evil. Westinghouse firmly grasped the scales of justice, and he went direct to Tesla and humbly told the story of his seeming defeat. Tesla quickly turned it into a spiritual triumph that will ring down through the years as a cosmic moment in which two men touched divinity

Standing there before Westinghouse, Tesla smiled serenely and tore up his contract without a trace of bitterness. At that moment he was entitled to at least twelve million dollars in royalties, but he tossed the scraps of his contract into the wastebasket. He had saved the Westinghouse organization, and Westinghouse would give his polyphase system to the world. The bankers could satisfy their love for money. Today this unfortunate planet is still reaping the black harvest from the seeds scattered far and wide by the bewitched money-men.

It has been said often that failure to pay royalties to Tesla proved to be the greatest handicap to scientific and industrial progress which the human race has ever experienced on this globe. In modern times the United States and all allied nations of the world are wondering why scientific superiority has been lost in recent years. The answer is simple. The pattern of events is not difficult to trace.

Karmic law was set in motion by the New York State Prison using Tesla's alternating-current invention to electrocute condemned prisoners. The karmic debt thus incurred precipitated at the point where alternating-current development was centered. Tesla was a White Magician and was protected against direct attack by the dark forces. He could be reached only indirectly. But the Westinghouse organization, through its money system, was wide open. The dark forces were able to attack freely through that open channel. This imperiled the work of Tesla. But since it was society that connived to support the prison authorities in their nefarious work, it is society that has had to suffer the karmic resuits. America allowed the Tesla inventions to be mis-used. It is America that must pay the karmic debt through a decline in scientific achievement.

A very few years after Tesla and Westinghouse made their historic decision, Tesla was a global intellectual giant of such stature that he could easily, with the use of his inventions and discoveries, have swung this planet from evil to goodness, from darkness to light, from ignorance to illumination. But society, in its utter complacency, preferred prison methods to the methods of a Venusian Initiate. And so the mills of the gods continued to grind slowly, awaiting the incoming seventh Ray which would bring the cleansing Violet Fire of transmutation to the Dark Star.

After the financial setback engineered by the Westinghouse money-men, Tesla never again had sufficient funds to develop his inventions. On many occasions his co-workers begged him to develop some small aspect of his inventions in order to make money to support his greater discoveries, but Tesla always refused to spend his time on what he termed small stuff. He had no desire to benefit a few people. He desired only to benefit humanity. Some of his co-workers felt that he was just being stubborn, but Tesla wisely knew his proper course.

When Tesla was nearly eighty years of age he was asked to give a speech before the Institute of Immigrant Welfare which, at a dinner meeting at the Hotel Biltmore on May 12, 1938, was to present the great inventor with an honorary citation. Tesla wrote out a speech which was read at the dinner because he did not feel equal to attending in person. He had not only survived through many, many years of extreme poverty, but he had been ridiculed for failing to commercialize his inventions. He was often unable to pay his hotel bills, and was forced to move frequently, leaving his luggage until friends could assist him to get settled in another lodging place.

Yet with this spectre of poverty always dogging at his heels, he gazed without rancor at a world which had waxed wealthy out of the power he had made available. And so on the occasion of the Biltmore dinner he paid tribute to Westinghouse in a magnificent testimonial to the heartfelt friendship which had always existed between the two men:

"George Westinghouse was, in my opinion, the only man on this globe who could take my alternating-current system under the circumstances then existing and win the battle against prejudice and money power. He was a pioneer of imposing stature, one of the world's true noblemen, of whom America may well be proud, and to whom humanity owes an immense debt of gratitude."

So it was at the age of 80 years that Tesla, the only man on the globe who could have invented alternating current, cited

George Westinghouse as the only man on the Dark Star who could have developed it, in spite of the pitiless and ruthless attacks by the forces of darkness, entrenched behind the money screen within his own company. Tesla declared his position as an Initiate in this statement about his friend, just as surely as did another Initiate who entered into the Temple and flayed the money-lenders with a whip.

As a Venusian Tesla was not karmically obliged to deal with money-lenders. His magnificent gesture of tearing up his own contract with Westinghouse showed that as a Venusian he was willing to go to any length to help his friend, knowing full well that Westinghouse was shouldering for all humanity a karmic burden so great that he could scarcely bear up under it. With the aid of Tesla's warm and enduring friendship he did bear up, giving Tesla's polyphase system to the world, thus eliminating a vast part of society's karmic debt. Tesla voiced a divine pronouncement when he stated that George Westinghouse was one of the world's true noblemen.

During the final years of his life, as he neared the age of 80, Tesla was aided by a $7,200 annual honorarium paid to him by the Yugoslav Government on behalf the Tesla Institute at Belgrade. As the hour of Tesla's birth approached, the spaceship on which he was born neared the earth in a mountain province that is now part of Yugoslavia. As the hour of his death approached, it was Yugoslavia that honored him and supported him financially.

The Tesla Institute was opened in Belgrade in 1936, in commemoration of Tesla's eightieth birthday. Formal celebrations were held throughout the country over a period of a week, honoring the greatest national hero the Yugoslavs had ever known. The Tesla Institute, endowed by both government and private sources, was equipped with a splendid research laboratory and library. Every bit of writing or information that had any bearing on Tesla and his inventions was collected and made available to research students at the Institute. American students have been deprived of any opportunity to learn about Tesla, because his name is seldom mentioned in school books, even science textbooks in the United States, the nation which

Tesla had honored with his citizenship, and the point from which his great inventions had rayed forth like light from a central sun.

Tesla passed his eightieth birthday quietly. He was interviewed and questioned about his World Wireless System for electrical distribution, a system which he had perfected many years before, and which rendered his polyphase system obsolete. He showed not the slightest sign of resentment over the fact that billions upon billions of dollars had been wasted by promoters in a greedy effort to extract the last penny of profit from an electrical system that was as outmoded as a dinosaur.

Tesla was comforted by his own inner joyous knowledge that he had not been called to share in commercial exploitations that needlessly sapped the wealth of the world. His philosophy of brotherhood, of friendship toward humanity, of gratitude toward his Creator, never wavered. And so he said, when questioned about his World Wireless System:

"Perhaps I was a little premature. We can get along without it as long as my polyphase system continues to meet our needs. Just as soon as the need arises, however, I have the system ready to be used with complete success."

It is still ready and it is still waiting to be used. Promoters are still withholding from the public the knowledge that such a system exists as an invention, waiting to be used. Promoters are still seeking to expand Tesla's obsolete polyphase system throughout the world, burdening the earth with miles upon miles of needless cables, conduits, wires and posts, providing dangerous playthings for high winds and blizzards. But this is the greedy method by which fortunes are made at the expense of the public.

In the New Age only new age methods will be utilized. Very soon now will come the big planetary housecleaning.

Then down will come all the cables, conduits, wires and posts, which the public is now paying to have installed. What fools these mortals be!

Since Otis T. Carr has now come forth with his free energy devices it is quite probable that Tesla, working from Shamballa, has in mind a system that will obsolete the World Wireless System. But at any rate, as Tesla said on his eightieth birthday, the system is there, waiting to be used with complete success if needed.

It calls for a small antenna device to be attached atop every house, office building, shop and factory. This device will enable the occupants of the building to have all the electricity they need without meters or wirings. The antenna will pick up a beamed supply of current, just as a radio picks up a broadcasted program. Inside the home or building the electrical service units such as lights, irons, stoves, adding machines, typewriters, and so forth, will be free from wires and plugs for wall outlets. The units will pick up the necessary current beamed from the antenna.

Even when Tesla had his old laboratories on South Main Street (now West Broadway) in New York, he had lights which could be picked up and placed in any position anywhere in the laboratory, wherever light happened to be needed at the moment. His lights were merely glass tubes, free from wires and wall fixtures.

So the inventor, for many years, enjoyed the fruits of his own inventions, while the public has paid and paid and paid the pipers who ever pipe for more money profits from their outmoded merchandise.

The Tesla wireless method for electrical distribution is a gift which the world might have utilized for the past half century had the public demanded it. But an uninformed public is a silent public. The public gets its information largely from newspapers and magazines, radio and TV. These sources are, in turn, controlled and censored by their advertisers and government secret-guarders. This conditioned public then dictates to its teachers and its preachers, telling them what to teach and what pulpit topics would be most uplifting to the community spirit. Thus the vicious circle whirls round and around like a satellite.

Even Tesla himself was told off by J. P. Morgan when he explained his world wireless system to the financier. Morgan listened to Tesla describe the glories of his invention, and then the money baron dismissed the whole subject as impractical because, as he pointed out, there would be no way of making money off the people if the people could have as much electricity as they wished by merely putting up a little antenna on their homes, or factories or office buildings.

Morgan further reminded Tesla that under the present system the manufacturers of wires, poles, and electrical installation equipment of all kinds, could make fortunes, and in addition, the electricity could be metered and everybody could be charged for every kilowatt they used. Tesla pointed out that electricity was free in the atmosphere, a free gift of God to His people, but such idealism naturally could not penetrate the thinking of a financier.

Early in the years when Tesla was training Otis T. Carr, he called Carr's attention to the same fact: electricity is free in the atmosphere, a gift of God to His people. Carr agreed with Tesla instantly. But Carr was not a financier. He was merely working as a clerk in a hotel package room. Perhaps therein lies the answer.

The OTC-XI

There is little doubt left in my mind, after having been in the military for so many years, that the Commander-in-Chief and those who pull his strings often do not tell even our very own fighting forces the "dirty little secrets" that could end the carnage in half the time. Since World War II our highest in command have been able to access the technical information that would have rendered the enemy senseless almost immediately, but because war has always been associated with "big business," they've usually felt it advantageous to the economy to let the battle drag on.

There is, for example, evidence that during the Persian Gulf War jet aircraft, capable of even more amazing maneuvers than the Stealth Bomber, were up in the air and upon occasion at the front lines, to scare the hell out of our foes. These noiseless craft can hover, beam down death dealing rays, and then pick up speed and disappear in a matter of a few seconds. They do not appear as targets on radar and their shapes are so different from what we are used to seeing in the sky that our enemies must certainly have thought that their god had betrayed them in favor of the American *devil*.

For the last couple of years we have been hearing some amazing stories coming out of a remote area in the Nevada desert known as Groom Lake or Area 51. At this site, the government is testing aerial devices that are as far advanced as those flown by Darth Vader's evil forces in the motion picture *Star Wars*. Some of the craft seen at this locale reportedly have the ability to skip across space and time; dematerializing and then popping up again in a different portion of the sky. Other craft have been seen to "split apart" in mid-air, and entire for-

94

mations have been sighted following across the desert like a freight train in the sky.

UFOs—as it seems fitting—have been an inspiration for many new age inventors who have looked toward the heavens for the secrets of gravity. The amazing ability of UFOs—in their many shapes and sizes—to fly about at incredible speeds and make incredible movements, has led these few "free thinking" souls to realize that all the laws of the universe have not—as yet —been discovered.

One such gentleman was Otis T. Carr of Baltimore, Maryland, who truly believed that humankind was only in its infancy as far as air flight goes, and that if we were ever to succeed in our endeavors to propel ourselves into space, ordinary rockets and the fuels they utilize would only lead to frustration, as they would never be able to properly do the job of moving civilization into the depths of space.

As it turns out, Carr was not only familiar with Tesla's work in the field of anti-gravity, but he actually met and spent some time with the great inventor—something few others can make a claim to. Based upon his own research and that which he learned from Tesla, Carr formed his own corporation in the late 1950s called OTC Enterprises, with the idea of building a space craft that could take us to the moon and beyond, quite economically and very safely. Margaret Storm best describes Carr's friendship with Nikola Tesla in these terms:

• • •

It was on a summer day in 1925 that Otis T. Carr was busy with his new duties as a package clerk in a large midtown hotel in New York. He had just arrived in the city to study art, and he found employment in order to cover his tuition. First, he was impelled to come to New York. Upon arrival, he felt impelled to apply for a job in a particular hotel. He was put to work at once and was just getting acquainted with his surroundings when Nikola Tesla wound his prophetic way through the subterranean passages of the lower basement and approached the new package clerk.

"When you finish your duties here," said Tesla with grave dignity, "go out and buy four pounds of unsalted peanuts and

95

bring them to my suite." He handed the lad from Elkins, West Virginia, sufficient money to cover the purchase, plus a generous gratuity. The gratuity was part of the Tesla legend; to him the laborer was very, very worthy of his hire.

Otis was not surprised at the nature of the request because, as he had often been told, in New York one could expect anything to happen. It was not in the least like Elkins. The package clerk carried out the order and delivered the peanuts to Tesla. Meanwhile, he made a few inquiries among the other clerks, and he found that Tesla was a great scientist who fed peanuts to pigeons. He even took care of the sick and injured pigeons and kept many of them in baskets upstairs in his suite.

Upon making the delivery, young Carr was invited by Tesla to come in for a chat. This was the beginning of one of the most unusual and fascinating stories of discipleship that has yet come to light in modern times. Usually people look upon the training of a disciple as something extremely mystical and esoteric, something that takes place within a lamasery or secluded retreat, far from the haunts of men and pigeons. But in this instance—and it is certainly one of the most successful instances of discipleship on record—most of the training took place on the steps of the New York Public Library.

Day after day, in good weather and bad, young Carr carried peanuts to Tesla. And day after day, the elderly scientist and his young protege strolled slowly along certain streets where flocks of pigeons were wont to gather in anticipation of the scattered nutmeats. The pilgrimage usually ended on the steps of the library on the west side, facing Bryant Park. There the two sat side by side, with Tesla urging the birds to eat out of his hand, while he explained to young Carr the fascinating details of their mysterious intelligence.

Tesla is said to have talked but little in those years, but fortunately young Carr was not inhibited by any knowledge of this fact. He asked the great genius so many questions and listened with such rapt eagerness to every syllable, that Tesla soon gave him a nickname—The Sponge. This served as a little joke between the two good friends, but actually the name was well chosen, as Tesla realized when he selected it.

Carr never saw Tesla again or had contact with him after the third year. During the thirty subsequent years, Carr spent hours daily in his own little workshop, performing the thousands of experiments that led to final success with the gravity motor and electric propulsion system. There in the workshop he found that he could, at any time, dip into the reservoir of his photographic memory, and bring forth in total recall every needed thought concerning sine wave or coil winding, or other Tesla applications and innovations.

Carr had no formal engineering training, nor had he any knowledge of esotericism before meeting Tesla. However, he was so inspired by the superman that he later steeped himself in philosophies of the east and the west, and ranged far and wide in his reading and studying, covering a vast field of knowledge. Like the martyred Bruno, Carr has come to be known as the academician without academy.

As he read and studied over the years, he always followed Tesla's example by going straight to the heart and brain of nature for his knowledge. He quickly discovered how to sort the absolutes from the mountains of dialectic chaff in the world's accumulated words and works. He never wasted precious time repeating what was proved.

As a result of his great perceptive guidance, it is estimated that Carr has advanced scientific achievement at least a century by concrete application of his free-energy discoveries. Like Tesla, he harbors no secrets about his inventions. He is more than happy to discuss them with anyone who will listen. Also, like Tesla, he has been unable thus far to sell them or even give them away.

Carr is a man who is characterized by an attitude of constant gratefulness. He is not only grateful to God and to Tesla, but his gratitude extends back to Archimedes and forward to Einstein, for he feels that the application of certain scientific principles down through the ages by countless discoverers and scientists, all contributed to his own inventions. This attitude is especially apparent in Carr's speech and writings. He stubbornly sticks to the plural form, we, in his narration of accomplishment.

When questioned about this he spoke of the total principles proved by the great men of history, and how each proof had entered into his final concept of the gravity motor and electrical accumulator. He acknowledges Archimedes' lever, Copernicus' constants, Galileo's acceleration, Newton's motions, Faraday's coil, Bacon's prerogatives, Edison's thermionics, Einstein's relativity, Franklin's static, Galvani's electrolysis, and Tesla's understanding of outer space; and the works of craftsmen like Fulton, Ford, and the Wright brothers, whose "follies, foibles, and infernal-machines" would never, it was said, perform the "fantasies" that are now commonplace.

Like Tesla, Carr desires that his inventions serve all humanity, not a privilege few. It is his wish that millions of individuals from all nations will have an opportunity to share in the development of the business as it unfolds. Aside from the fact that he is definitely opposed to any monopolistic practices, his corporate structure is not unlike that of other successful world producers.

The basic design for all his business stationery, brochures, booklets, and so forth, is not only interesting and original, but extremely symbolic. His initials, OTC, are arranged so as to form the sign of Omega. Surmounting this is the White Dove—Tesla's Dove—in full, graceful flight. Below is the motto which reads: Peace and plenty through the application of free energy to supply all things to all people.

Carr has already met the same resistance from the forces of darkness that plagued Tesla, and, as usual, it comes through money channels and threats of economic boycott—this time in relation to newspaper advertising. In launching an announcement of his inventions, Carr had a full-page advertisement prepared for insertion in a leading daily paper of Baltimore. The advertisement was paid for and accepted by the paper. Shortly thereafter it was cancelled by the newspaper and the money refunded. The newspaper had to cancel the advertising at the request of one of their big money-spenders who had metered power, not free energy, for sale to the public. Therefore, the people of Baltimore and vicinity were not informed of free-energy devices capable of powering everything from a hearing aid to a spaceship.

While the governments still deny the existence of flying saucers, and daily newspapers refuse to give outstanding news to their readers in the form of a paid advertisement, uniformed public remains uninformed. They do not even know that the problem of space flight has been solved by an American citizen. They are not even told that it is now possible to power everything with free energy drawn from the atmosphere; that we need no longer be enslaved by petroleum, coal and old forms of fuel.

Silence Group

This is news of world importance, yet so strict is the gangster censorship imposed by the Silence Group, that newspapers founded for the purpose of giving news to the public dare not carry out their function, for to do so would mean running the risk of ruinous economic sanctions. However, Carr and his associates displayed no resentment over the refusal of the daily newspaper to carry the advertising. Instead, they placed page ads in small suburban weeklies which were overjoyed to have the sudden business windfall.

The result was not only amazing, but proved conclusively that the public wanted to be informed about Carr's inventions. From far and wide, letters of inquiry began to pour in. Hundreds of extra copies of the newspapers were requested to be sent to relatives and friends in distant states and countries. Requests for literature on the Carr machines reached huge proportions, and continued to soar day after day. Scores of people sent in small amounts of money—from a dollar to five dollars—as a down payment on stock that was not even offered for sale. Visitors began to arrive with requests for information on everything from vast power plants to spaceships.

Meanwhile, Carr offered to build and deliver space ships to governments wishing to send expeditions to the moon or elsewhere, but these offers were declined in favor of much more expensive rocket and missile programs.

This is a most interesting and intriguing development. The space people have stated that they will not permit military or tourist landings on the moon. The Hierarchy has announced that no individual in an unascended body can make a trip into outer space. If governments do not believe in the existence of flying saucers from outer space, then they cannot accept the fact that the space people have a station on the moon. Why, then, do they hesitate to use a Carr spaceship to go to the moon, and find out for themselves what is up there?

It seems obvious that they do know there is a space station on the moon. Undoubtedly, the space people have told them that they will not be permitted to land, and they know that space people mean business. In the meantime they can keep on playing with their rocket toys in order to fool the taxpayer, and give the impression that he is getting something big and grand for his money.

Carr is not planning to have a large spaceship ready for flight for at least a year [as of the time the book was written— Editor]. It is quite possible that he could make a trip to the moon and be permitted to land there. Inasmuch as he would be testing his own ship, the trip would have no military significance, and he is entirely in accord with the program set up by the space people. Also, by the time he has a ship of sufficient size ready for a voyage into outer space, it might be possible for him to make that trip too, especially if one or more space persons would agree to accompany him. But these conjectures are entirely unique and apply only to Carr.

What he can or cannot accomplish has nothing to do with the attitudes of governments which first refuse to admit the possibility of spaceships from other planets and then refuse to try out a local model. Supposing it is not entirely successful on the trial run? It certainly could not be less successful than many of the rockets and satellites which the government is attempting to launch at the expense of the taxpayers. Furthermore, a rocket leads but to destruction. A spaceship leads to the freedom of the cosmic highways and opens a vast new universe to the wonderment of man.

Since Carr's free energy devices are designed to power anything from a hearing aid to a spaceship, it is clear why his advertising is refused by daily newspapers, and why the government refuses to even try a Carr spaceship on the national budget— just one size, at least. Carr's free-energy motors will power automobiles, for one thing—a development which would do away with the need for gasoline, and as an added advantage do away with smelly exhaust fumes.

For years, geologists and scientists have been bemoaning the fact that our natural fuels such as petroleum will soon be exhausted. They have painted grim word pictures of a shivering, stranded populace, hovering over a meager fire of sticks and twigs, and just about to perish for lack of fuel. Yet when Otis T. Carr announces free-energy motors the newspapers hasten to keep the whole thing hush-hush lest the people find out that they will not have to shiver after all.

There is still another reason why the Silence Group, operating through black disciples in the military and commercial business arenas, has decreed that Carr's inventions should be played down. Carr is obviously working on behalf of the Forces of Light and he is probably the first man in history who has had the courage to incorporate that theme in his paid newspaper advertising.

He is irrevocably against mistreatment of the atom, for well he knows that an atom is God's handiwork, and a tiny pulsing life. In the advertisement he states that his machines are natural machines; that they produce unlimited energy without fission, without fusion, and without violence of any kind. They do not smash the atom. They do not split the atom. They do not blast the atom.

He reminds his readers that his machines are profoundly simple devices that collect and direct the free and boundless energies of the sun "in the same way the sun's energies cause the earth to spin and rivers to flow, the bread to rise and the plants to grow, and the great ocean tides to rise and fall." He states that the accumulator uses the sun's force of electromagnetism by means of natural reproductive chemistry, and that the motor is powered entirely by the sun's immutable pressure energy known as gravity.

He sums up not only his method by his philosophy as follows:
All energy is atomic
The light from the sun
The pull of gravity
The fission of uranium
The fusion of hydrogen
All that moves
Or grows, or glows

Everywhere on earth
And throughout the Universe.
It is all atomic energy.

Its utrionic presence is everywhere,
being even Nature itself.

And held in plain view for all
the time we know, it has yet
remained Nature's closest secret.

So, how to borrow of this energy
from Nature, has been quite
a problem.

When you *fight* Nature,
Nature *always* fights back.

If we try to share Nature's energy
by injuring Nature, we will only
injure ourselves accordingly.

Try to change the weather in one
place and you get storms, or floods,
or drought in another.

Crack or split the atom and you
get frightful devastation or
poisonous radiation.

And while you may blast a dog or
a man away into space, you will
never safely blast him back again.

We know the laws of Nature do not
change, so why waste the effort
and take the terrible risks?

There is only one right way.
The right way is the peaceful way.
And we have found the way!

Carr's architectural plans for a Space Research Institute to be located at Space, Maryland, have been drawn up, and preliminary construction activities are under way on a beautiful plot of land of about 70 acres outside Baltimore. The new post office will be called Space.

Space Research Institute is expected to become the world center for activities connected with spaceships, interplanetary travel, interplanetary communication, and a better way of life through the utilization of natural solar energy devices. The group of buildings incorporate new design motifs which should make them outstanding in architectural beauty.

Although Space Research Institute will serve as headquarters for the Otis T. Carr Enterprises, he does not plan to mass-manufacture any of his devices. The institute, as its name implies, is strictly for research. There the group will design prototypes of machines which will then be turned over to other manufacturers to be produced in quantity. Mr. Carr has behind him the long history of Tesla's frustrated attempts to make the world a more comfortable place in which to live, and to give humanity countless hours of leisure time for study and evolutionary advancement. Therefore, his primary interest is not in becoming a manufacturer himself, but in the opportunity of all industry, the world over, to share in the ownership and distribution of products patterned after the basic prototypes.

Since Carr is a disciple of Tesla, and since Tesla refused to participate in the conniving, competitive commercial manipulations of his day, businessmen everywhere are eager to know how Carr, faced with problems almost identical to those of Tesla, plans to surmount the many obstacles which are certain to be placed in his way by the forces of darkness. The answer seems to be contained within the utilitarian functions of the inventions themselves. Once the public knows that the devices will provide a better way of life, it is up to the public to demand that the inventions be made available.

The OTC circular-foil spacecraft looks and operates like a flying saucer. The first experimental models will be anywhere from forty to a hundred feet in diameter, and will cost millions of dollars, as do first prototypes of any aircraft. However, one small model, ten feet in diameter will be constructed for special test purposes in actual usage.

Unlike conventional aircraft, the large space vehicles will soon be brought down to family size of about ten feet in diameter. They can be built to sell for less than the cost of a modern automobile, and are designed to take a family across town, across the nation, or around the world in absolute comfort and safety, and in a fraction of the time ever before possible. Carr expect[ed] to be ready during 1959 to start licensing manufacturers all over the world to mass-produce the OTC space vehicles in many sizes and styles for every transportation need.

It is Mr. Carr's sincere opinion that the introduction, manufacture, and use of the free-energy devices will bring more prosperity to more people in the United States and around the globe, than any single invention in the entire history of the world. He realizes that most of the world's problems today have their roots in hunger for more energy than is available.

"States and nations are already fighting over what is left of ordinary fuels and the available supplies of water to make electricity and irrigate the land," states Mr. Carr. "We have had many recent examples of the delicate balance of supply and demand, even in this great country. We've seen the rationing of gasoline and oil. We've seen the lights go dim in the Pacific Northwest.

"We've seen vast millions of burning desert acres barren only for lack of a little irrigation. And now even the oilmen are beginning to squeeze the last drop out of every ton of shale.

"The power hunger is the same the world over, only it is more intense now. The most shocking recent example was the willingness of Egypt to close the Suez Canal and fight the world for a few kilowatts of electricity.

"Free-energy devices can change all this in a remarkably short space of time. Enough electric power and energy in the right places, and we will have undreamed of markets for every other kind of goods and materials and appliances our factories and shops can turn out.

"And so goes the simple formula: Give the world enough electrical energy, and you raise the world's standard of living. Raise the world's standard of living, and you raise the world's economy.

"The best way to get the total concept of what free energy means to the world today, is to suppose that the wheel were just now being discovered. Then visualize the free-energy motor putting the wheel into the air, into an entirely new dimension. Industry must realize that these devices will provide power for automobiles, trains, great ocean liners, and spaceships, as well as for such things as hearing aids, portable television sets, refrigerators, and will even furnish power, light, and heat for large cities or communities.

"Our free-energy devices will do all these things by perpetual space-forces of magnetism, gravity, and electro-magnetism—and by these forces alone; forces which are free and available everywhere on the face of the earth and throughout the universe.

While the world is still groveling under the ancient edict that called for earning one's bread by the sweat of one's brow, the question of how free-energy devices will affect employment is a paramount one. But Mr. Carr feels that his inventions and discoveries truly represent the inception of a basic new industry, which for sheer size and scope might be properly compared with the steel, automobile and aircraft industries combined. He believes that pioneering in free energy will automatically introduce a new concept of employment practices and employee relationships.

Although the space people themselves have had no contact with Otis T. Carr and have had no direct hand in his work, it is safe to assume that they have been watching it carefully. In addition, Tesla and Dove have assuredly directed it from the scientific department of Shamballa, making certain that it will fit into the Divine Plan at exactly the right moment. This, then, is the right moment.

• • •

From what we were told at the time, the principle his saucer-shaped craft was to utilize was, he said, relatively simple, mainly taking electrical power from the air. This power was the same "free energy" that caused the Earth to rotate on its axis and orbit around the sun and could turn a machine described as two cones joined at their circular basis. When the rotation of such a machine reached a certain velocity relative to the Earth's orbital velocity, Carr said it would take off.

Carr's principles were realistically close to those that Nikola Tesla spoke of harnessing. We said *was* since Mr. Carr has long since vanished (he has most likely passed away) after having to battle with Uncle Sam who, initially, seemed fascinated with Carr's work and offered to partially finance the project, but later dropped out and ended up prosecuting Carr on an apparently trumped up charge of selling securities in OTC Enterprises without a proper license.

According to published accounts, Carr's proposition to the government was that "OTC Enterprises would build a working craft, circular in design and approximately 45 feet in diameter by 15 feet in height, with a crew compartment that would accommodate at least three persons in comfort under conditions encountered to within one thousand miles from the Earth. The craft would depart from any specified location in the continental United States, orbit one or two times outside the Earth's atmosphere, and land its crew safely within the inner rotunda courtyard of the Pentagon Building in Washington, or at any other location best suited to public observation. The craft would be powered "from natural environmental sources acting in motion-concert with self-contained chemical components of the Utron power-package and needing no additive, servicing or replacement prior to at least one year of operation in our atmosphere."

Carr was the first to acknowledge the fact that much of his information on anti-gravity was received "through intelligent guidance by one's guardian Deity. My guidance led me to learn the life-span conclusions that had been reached before my time by all the true philosophers who observed and discerned and recorded the immutable laws of universal truths."

One of Carr's confessions was that his OTC-X1 was to be constructed "from well-known basic principles that stem from the works of the Einsteins and Teslas, and the dozens of other free thinkers who held truth and integrity above all material gain or loss."

A philosopher as well as an inventor, Carr said that "Essentially what I have done is collect, arrange, adapt and orchestrate some of Nature's compositions into harmonious assemblage.

"They are fashioned out of God's creation.

"They are instruments of space.

"Their music is for all the worlds of man."

Here is how one of Carr's promotional releases described the OTC-X1, "truly a spacecraft that is the first true terrestrial spacecraft of this age—using space itself as the catalyst for the interchangeable forces of electromagnetism and gravity."

The OTC X-1

While most observers regard Mr. Carr's inventions as great miracles of ingenuity, their greatest asset is the fact that they are miracles of simplicity.

In looking to nature for his guidance, as he was first inspired to do by the oracles of Sir Francis Bacon, Otis T. Carr observed while still a very young man, that natural systems, though they may appear complex, are never complicated.

The forms of movements of universal bodies are geometrically precise—their movements constant and orderly.

The motions and directions of universal energies are ever predictable in dimension, frequency, and velocity.

So after he had learned enough of these basics, in about 1938, Mr. Carr began to design his Spaceforms as miniature reproductions of natural, universal systems.

As you look at the electro-gravitational power-package of the OTC-X1, in the phantom view [in this chapter] for example, wherein all the essential components are shown within the hull environment, you will see what is in effect a miniature solar system.

Let us say by analogy, that the Utron electrical accumulator in the center is the Sun of this system. Within its physical material walls of curvilinear dissimilars there pulsates an electrochemical heart of a billion-billion atomic and subatomic hatcheries that are its inertial energy potential. Each a translation of nature's universal miracles, each of complex simplicity, and each ever ready to supply a part of the pressure energy that will take the OTC-X1 wherever man chooses to travel throughout God's vast Universe.

From this heart system, within the Utron, electromotive forces are conducted to the copper wire coils of the planetary field-magnets, there are twelve in this drawing, spaced equidistant from each other integrally around the periphery of the lower hull-section.

The excitation of forces between the pole faces of the magnets establishes a condition of uni-polarization between the magnets and the capacitor plates, which you see formed around the structural insulator of the central disc-assembly.

The consequent pressure energy of these uni-polarized space-forces gives an equal and opposite push against the two opposing assemblies (one being the hull, the other the center disc) and causes them to rotate counter to each other with equal velocity. As soon as this motion starts, the Utron regenerative-armature coils, six in this drawing, mounted on trunnion shafts through their opposing vortexial axis, immediately begin to complete the cycle of mutation and transmutation of matter and energy by which the forces that first emanated from the central accumulator are returned to their relatively static inertial balance.

So in both appearance and function, our OTC-X1 Space-craft is a miniature facsimile of the planets, the moons, the stars, and the energies in the unified field of the natural systems around us.

By obeying instead of violating the Universal natural laws under which our systems operate, we are able to regulate the course and relative velocity of our craft in its travels, either from one terrestrial city to another, or out on lengthy visits into the unexplored reaches of the great beyond.

For it is true of universal space as it is true of our own ocean waters, that the immutable laws of mass-displacement will let our OTC Spacecraft ride the magneto-gravito waves—as buoyant as the liners ride the Atlantic.

And even more so.

Electrical flight in the OTC-X1 Spacecraft will transcend all of man's prior experiences with the transportation devices of our time in many ways other than speed, velocity, and distance.

While it is true that we will soon learn to regard a million earth-miles-an-hour as an interplanetary snail's pace, we will also learn that man need experience no annoyance or discomfort either in or out of this earth's atmosphere.

As your eyes take in the shapes and relationships in these illustrations of the miniature model you're about to build, your reasoning will let you understand much about the invisible forces that contribute to the noise-free, pressure-free, and vibrationless sensation of floating flight to be experienced in the passenger living rooms aboard the OTC-X1. It will be very much like reclining in an overstuffed armchair on our comfortable old planet earth.

Its mechanical behavior being like that of a giant gyroscope, and electrically like a planet with its own atmosphere and force-field, the OTC-X1 will know nothing of sound barriers, shockwaves, skin friction, turbulence, or "G-strains."

Neither will it or its occupants need fear any harm from cosmic forces, Gamma-rays, X-rays, or other radiation, because the OTC-X1 craft will be either using or absorbing all such forces, or by the pressure and polarity of its own force field, be shielded against their penetration.

While the commutation system for the actual energized flight-model craft is not shown together with the other components on this sheet, its design for the circuitry of electro-gravitational forces permits an environmental surroundment of equal and opposite pressures in and from all directions, whose circumference is nowhere and whose center is everywhere relative to the universal field.

Thus, by imitating nature, we become one with nature—by translating her shapes and duplicating her motions we join forces with natural energies and become magnificently independent of man-made limitations, man-constructed barriers, man-invented fears, and man-imposed controls!

And with the flick of a switch, at speeds too dazzling for human observation, we can with hairline precision alter our course to any desired direction by interposing artificial variable resistances among the natural forces of pressure in differential relationships to the tensor-stress contacts within any system of the universal force-field.

THE TESLA SCOPE FOR SPACE COMMUNICATION

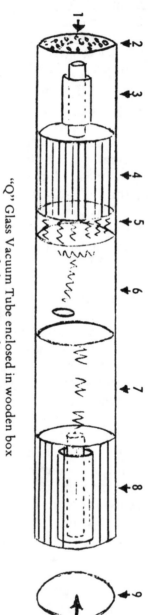

"Q" Glass Vacuum Tube enclosed in wooden box
9 ft. long, 5" in diameter

Legend:
(1) Audio Output. (2) Pick up. (3) Converter. (4) Automatic Control Chamber.
(5) Gas Chamber. (6) Converter. (7) Received Energy Control. (8) Dark Room (this
section enclosed in pure silver shield). (9) Head.

TESLA'S CONCEPTION OF THE EARTH/ATMOSPHERE AS A GIANT ELECTRICAL CAPACITOR

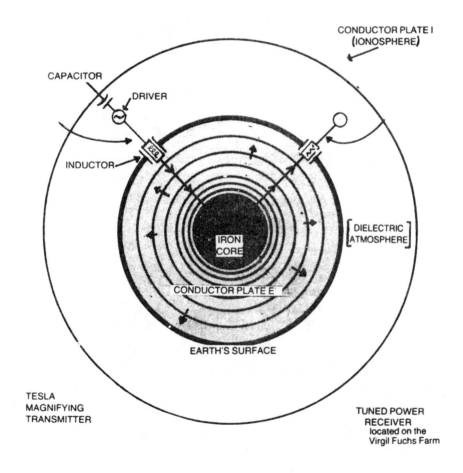

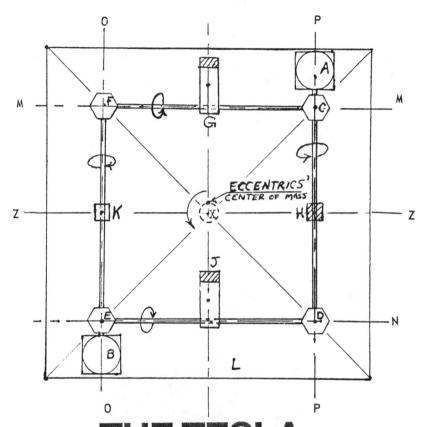

THE TESLA SPACE DRIVE

Key:

A and B are motors (should be identical)

C, D, E and F are right-angle drives 1:1 ratio

G, H, J, and K are eccentrics

L is the base plate to which the motors, gear boxes, and pillow blocks (not shown) are fastened

M, N, O, and P are the axes of rotation of eccentrics G, H, J, and K

Y and Z are the planes of rotation of the eccentrics

X is the line of intersection of planes Y and Z

This, then, is the route past all limits of the horizon, a breakthrough that brushes aside all artificial obstruction in any form.

It is as predicted in Bacon's prefatory remark several hundred years ago when he published his Novum Organum,

"If man would conquer Nature

"Man must join with Nature."

The inventions of Otis T. Carr, and their development for the world's free commerce and industry by the OTC Enterprises, will mark man's attainment of the ultimate employment of Nature's forces.

The Utron electrical accumulator, and the Carrotto gravity motor will make electricity a willing slave to do man's chores, carry him where he wants to go, and light the roads along his way. These two OTC devices, developed and applied in peaceful service to humanity, will lift you and all of today's generations of man into a new heritage of free abundance.

It is all yours to grasp and hold for a good life of free expression, free communication, and the free pursuit of opportunity.

It is the promise fulfilled of:

"Peace and Plenty Through

"The Application Of Free Energy

"To Supply All Things For All People."

● ● ●

Carr also released illustrations of his spacecraft and the powers that propelled it along with more information on what he hoped to accomplish. He also broke the news about the Carrotto Gravity Motor, the Photon Gun and other aspects of his work.

Carr's Announcement: Carrotto Dynamics Inc. Introduces the Carrotto Gravity Motor

We have introduced the CARROTTO GRAVITY MOTOR as an electrical engine. It has many other applications. A compressor motor to build up pressure in hydraulics will surely be one essential application; and of course, it has a wide application in all forms of mechanical use aside from electricity. Our investigation of the atom in the middle thirties led us to this novel discovery. Here you will see the first physical correlation of natural forces at work in four-dimensional application.

You need only look around you to see the need for many fruitful applications of this new controlled-energy source which may never be practical with the massive devices now being built and planned around reactors using fusion and fission procedures to derive power from the atom.

The Carrotto Gravity Motor is *portable*. It requires no fixed location or large building in which to function.

The Carrotto Gravity Motor is *flexible*. It can be made in whatever size best suits the purpose of the application.

The Carrotto Gravity Motor is *safe*. It requires no massive shielding to protect people from deadly radiation.

The Carrotto Gravity Motor is *limitless*. It can produce whatever power is desired for practical application on earth or in space.

The applications of the mighty, unlimited power described in part on these pages must be handled with caution and great care, for economic reasons.

We are aware that any and all inventions in the physical world eventually result in betterment for all of society. We are also aware that radical changes can cause undue hardship on established operations that have reached a peak in our economy during a long steady growth.

There has always been a great hue and cry from the leaders of the work force that new discoveries would cause great hardship to masses of people through unemployment. Within our memory we have read or heard that everything from the cotton-gin to the electronic computer would cause economic catastrophe. None of this has come to pass. Each and every new device of modern commerce and industry has created new fields of endeavor with new and larger employment opportunities for everyone.

Today's proportion of per-capita employment and per-capita share of gross national product is at an all-time high.

In fact, we have reached a turning point at which we must begin to wonder where tomorrow's employables will come from to man the desks and machines for future supply in an expanding economy.

A generally accepted prognosis of the next 25 years is that, "White collar workers will be far more numerous...people who

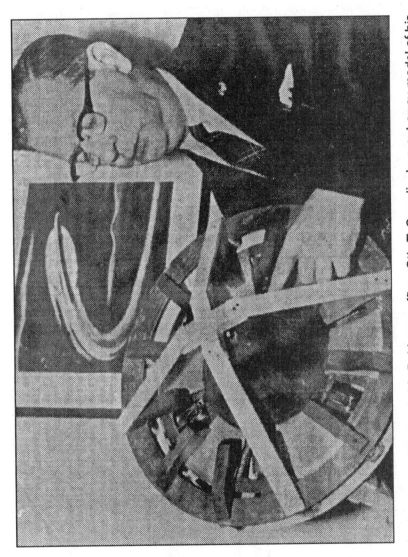

In a rare picture taken in his Baltimore office, Otis T. Carr displays cut away model of his craft, indicating the rotation principle that would enable the OTC-X1 to rise into space.

run things will be almost double in number. Population will go up some 20% by 1967 (50% in 25 years) [How true this has been, when viewed from the perspective of the 1990s—Editor], but the number of people available to work will increase only about 5% or 6%. This trend is manifest throughout the world.

As a consequence...the pressure to produce more with fewer people...will affect all business planning.

OTC Enterprises will be a powerful factor in the new balance between man and the machine. New opportunities will be opened for the educated white-collar workforce of course, and for as many of such as our schools and colleges can produce. But even more important—WE WILL REPLACE THE NEED FOR THE BRUTE ENERGY FOR WHICH THE WORLD HAS TOO LONG LEANED ON—THE RAPIDLY DISAPPEARING BLUE-COLLAR AND NO-COLLAR WORKER.

We will not stop until we have penetrated our great discoveries into all the ends of the earth, or even as far into outer space as man desires to go!

The Photon Gun

A unique reaction wherein the controlled direction of radiant energy can be applied into an acceleration of mass approaching the velocity of light itself. This is primarily a development for use outside the earth's atmosphere. We are entering the age of space flight, and the use of solar energy in such is practically unlimited.

There is great simplicity in designs that refract light. We cannot show the same here without undue disclosures. Our experiments and investigations have made known to us that the mighty power from the Sun can be utilized when the geometry of design is properly evaluated. We are aware of the resistance factors involved, due to the earth's atmosphere, and our developments have been predicated on overcoming these, which in some instances has been done.

We Have Invented A Fourth Dimensional Space Vehicle

This Fourth Dimensional Vehicle is powered by the revolutionary Utron electric accumulator, which is completely round

Public relations spokesperson Major Wayne S. Aho shows OTC-X1 model at OTC Ceremonial Dinner in Oklahoma City.

and completely square, and generates its own power, which is electro-magnetism and electromotive force. It can be launched from the earth, and does not have to be blasted into space. The basic design was brought to the attention of the United States Government, and a patent application was filled in 1949.

Some tests were independently made by qualified engineers at one of America's leading plants and it was estimated that a small model, only four inches in diameter, produced energy equivalent to 1,000 tons. This was in 1952, and Mr. Carr was unable to interest anyone in his efforts at that time. Things have changed, and the Government has now put its blessing on space-flight development.

At the present time the rocket enthusiasts are commanding topmost attention. But there will be changes in thinking, and new directions of endeavor very soon. Our experiments with circular-foil design, as relates to gravity, electro-magnetism, and electromotive force, have led us to the certain conclusion that it is possible to use the inverse-proportion laws of Newton as successfully as the third law of motion applies to accelerated rockets. We will produce the OTC-X1 circular-foil spacecraft as the first operational prototype as symbolized in this conception drawing.

Revised Bulletin
We Have Won The Race Into Outer Space

There is much talk about Rockets and Missiles and about the years and money it will take to get to the Moon and back or to make a platform where we can watch over our "enemies."

The total answer to space travel has long been contained in our pertinent summation of physical law that: "Any vehicle accelerated to an axis rotation relative to its attractive inertial mass immediately becomes activated by free space-energy and acts as an independent force."

This is the equation that can get us to the Moon or wherever else in the solar system we want to go—at small cost and without blasting ourselves off the face of the earth.

We have twenty years of research and know-how and will build our OTC spacecraft for peaceful travel and transportation. Yet it is a plain fact that the OTC-X1 *is* the ULTIMATE MIS-

1964 Presidential candidate Gabriel Green keeps feet on the ground by the nearly completed 45 foot educational and recreational space replica of the OTC-X1

SILE because being manned in outer space, it can pick off any other device now being made or planned, and is now being offered to the United States Military for whatever purpose they choose to use it!

Meantime, OTC Enterprises will proceed with its plans for peaceful manufacture of free-energy systems and manned spacecraft in the belief that Americans under God can equal or surpass the technology of any nation on earth.

Otis T. Carr, President
O.T.C. Enterprises, Inc.

• • •

On April 19, 1959, a model of the OTC-X1 was put on display at Frontier City in Oklahoma. It was mistakenly believed by some that it was meant to fly, though it was really being presented as an "educational and recreational space ride," and was never meant to take a crew into space.

At around the time the prototype of the craft was revealed to the public, Carr was taken ill from what was believed to be a burst blood vessel in the upper right lung caused by over-work and strain. We are told that scientists worked day and night for "24 hour stretches trying to get all the assembly complete for a preliminary pre-flight rotation" that was to be televised nationally. Unfortunately, "a leak developed in the seam of the accumulator spraying mercury through the mechanism, and making it necessary to disassemble and clean all parts."

Carr has vanished from the scene, and is rumored to be deceased. But his work will not be forgotten. Somewhere out there, hopefully, someone has retained his life's work and will some day present a work model of the OTC-X1 to the world.

This is an actual photo of the first six-foot prototype of the OTC-X1 Electro-Gravitic spacecraft that was to be launched but never did because of illness on the part of the inventor and repeated harassment by the government. (Photo by Gabriel Green.)

Tesla, God And Arthur H. Matthews

Few people can claim to have known Tesla personally, and damn few can say that they were an actual associate of this great individual. One exception is an elderly Canadian gentleman by the name of Arthur H. Matthews, who initially surfaced at an unlikely place, when he went public at a UFO conference held in Paris, with the fact that he had successfully been using the Tesla Scope since 1947 to communicate with extraterrestrials.

Quiet and secluded, Matthew's property in Quebec had become a landing pad for spaceships, who descended onto his property in the middle of the night without being observed by the curious.

The Space Brothers who came in the wee hours ably continued Matthew's education program begun by Tesla, and even warned the scientist many years ago that the Russians were manufacturing their version of the *Tesla Sphere,* a powerless aircraft that Nikola had originally designed as far back as 1917.

Tesla knew that the knowledge he had was potentially dangerous if released onto a world that was not spiritually ready for it. It is said that when Tesla arrived from space as a child, he already knew what his task was to be, and had to select only those whom he felt could help the whole of humankind and not just themselves.

Margaret Storm, who had the opportunity to spend considerable time with Arthur H. Matthews, reveals that Tesla was charged with the task of bringing wireless or radio communication to the attention of a forgetful humanity, as well as television. "He then confided to Matthews," says Storm, "precise instructions for the building of the interplanetary communications set. Beyond that point it was not necessary or even prudent for Tesla to reveal the ultimate plans for communication."

Furthermore, when Tesla tried to get various governments to accept his "anti-war machine" in 1935, and failed, he personally asked Matthews to continue work on the design and to perfect it.

In the papers she left the world, Margaret Storm gives this personal account of Arthur H. Matthew's continuing work on behalf of Tesla and the tribulations associated with what he is trying to accomplish.

• • •

Margaret Storm's Account:

Arthur Matthews was a boy in England and his father, an electrical engineer, was working there with Lord Kelvin, when he first met Tesla. Kelvin had become interested in Tesla's wonderful new discovery of wireless or radio, and had invited Tesla to come to England to discuss the subject. It was there that the lifelong friendship began between Tesla and the Matthews', father and son. The three worked together until the death of Mr. Matthews, the father, in 1915. Then Arthur Matthews carried on until Tesla left the physical plane in 1943, and has continued the activity since.

During his last years, Tesla turned over a vast amount of material to Matthews in trust and confidence. He had in earlier years inspired Otis T. Carr to pursue 30 years of basic research leading to the present development of the Carr free-energy devices and the Carr spaceship.

In fact, when Tesla died in New York City on the night of January 7, 1943, it was generally assumed that his earthly work was finished. The forces of darkness rejoiced at news of his death which they considered most opportune. The world was at war and under pressure of this need the patents of Tesla were considered as royal plunder. The government agents moved in swiftly and seized all papers that Tesla had left in his safe, never suspecting that the incomparable genius had left them there merely to satisfy the idle curiosity of nosy people.

Later, after due inspection and after World War II, most of the papers were considered of such little value that they were turned over to the Tesla Institute in Belgrade, despite the fact that Tito was in power in that country. The Yugoslav Institute recently published, in English, a very impressive volume that they indicate is definitive, and which lists about 85 Tesla patents, together with reprints of some of his lectures and a brief story of his life.

However, Arthur Matthews is acquainted with at least 1,200 inventions, very important inventions, perfected by Tesla. He is only amused when he inspects recently published volumes, such as the Yugoslav book and another new American book, purporting to set forth the true facts about Tesla. These researchers have scraped the bottom of the barrel trying to turn up Tesla's inventions, but they all seem to stop when they reach No. 85, falling 1,115 short of the correct total.

Many top-flight scientists seek out Arthur Matthews these days in a belated attempt to "pump" him for information about Tesla's discoveries. But Arthur Matthews wisely keeps his own counsel; he also keeps the confidence and trust that Tesla bestowed upon him. However, the scientists do not go away empty-handed. Mr. Matthews gives to each and every one a sound piece of advice that he, himself, has tested over the years, and which he has found to be the ultimate goal for all seekers.

"Every time we wish to do something," he says, "we should go to God first for wisdom, because He is the Author of all science. Tesla was able to accomplish so much and see into the future because he understood God. From my own personal contacts with the space people, I find that their advancement is due to their faith and their obedience to Divine Law."

The Communists Arrive

The scientists who visit Matthews usually arrive heavily burdened with many university degrees and much learning, but, as they confess, they somehow missed Tesla and now they would like to know something about him. Tucked under their arms is the new communist-issued volume on Tesla that they have just purchased in order to bone up on the subject of the great scientist who did his major work in the United States. But something is either wrong with them or wrong with the book, because the two cannot get together. So they trek all the way to Quebec, and far beyond Quebec, out into the deep countryside of lakes and forests, in order to seek out Matthews in the hope of casting some light on the subject of Tesla's theories, which they admit they cannot grasp.

Mr. Matthews receives them in his serene and cordial way, and then he tells them, as kindly as he can, "If you would understand Tesla, you must first attune your mind to God." Since the unfortunate scientists usually know less about God than they know about Tesla, the result is confusion confounded.

Forces of Darkness

The forces of darkness, especially in the United States, have become very active in their efforts to suppress the truth about Tesla. Matthews and Carr have been ridiculed repeatedly, and often by the very scientists and government officials who sought their advice. The present author has received hundreds upon hundreds of letters praising her efforts, but she has received a few telling her she is just plain crazy. The writers do not explain why they think so, but they just think so. Oddly enough, these critical letters, so naive they might have been written by a somewhat retarded schoolboy, come only from men who call themselves experts and authorities.

They are experts, to be sure, but it must be clearly understood that they are experts in working for the dark forces only; they are authorities on the subject of evil; they are the chosen tools of the black magicians who roamed the astral plane freely, and even the physical plane, until just before the opening days of World War II, when they met their come-uppance from the Forces of Light.

Arthur H. Matthews clearly declared the depth of his dedication to New Age developments when he advised seekers to go straight to God, as Tesla had done. Tesla did not fear change, even when it meant that his new inventions would obsolete his earlier ones. Nor did he ever attempt to harbor secrets concerning his discoveries. Arthur Matthews has pointed out that the lectures that Tesla gave in London and in America between the years 1889 to 1894 contain all the information that is needed to construct virtually all devices patented by Tesla. These lectures have been collected and printed in book form, and have been available at least in all major libraries throughout the western world since the turn of the century. Yet hundreds of readers have scanned them and passed them by as interesting but not practical.

Mr. Matthews attributes this lack of realism to the darkness in which men's minds are immersed—the darkness of materialism. He says that Tesla's lectures cannot be understood by those whose minds are not attuned to God. Matthews actually tested out this theory in the presence of top-flight scientists and engineers who visited him to inspect the Tesla set for interplanetary communication.

These men looked at the set; they asked questions that were frankly answered. Mr. Matthews even went beyond that point and gave several hints, but not one seeker could even guess at the underlying scientific principles that Tesla had discovered and which made the set possible.

Yet these same scientists and engineers, and hundreds more of their kind, are the very men who are called into government service and who are supported by the taxpayers. They are presumed to have sufficient intelligence to handle whatever scientific problems arise in the course of their work. Yet the greater part of their energy is expended in trying to maintain an attitude of secrecy so that the long-suffering taxpayers will not find out the cold scientific facts advanced by Tesla even before the year of 1900.

How many Americans know that Tesla designed the Sphere, a powerless aircraft that the Allies might have used to end World War I even before November, 1918; and that might have been used to launch an air age 40 years ago, that would have rivaled the jet age of 1958? And how many Americans know even today that Tesla had designed another aircraft far superior to the Sphere, and that he actually built a model of it in 1893?

And how many people in the world today realize that Tesla knew all about cosmic rays long before the turn of the century, and that in 1891, Tesla built a cosmic ray engine, a free-energy device, to utilize the rays, which, like God and electricity, are everywhere? Just as an electric generator by force or by some other action brings electricity into motion, so did Tesla's cosmic ray engine bring the rays into motion.

Tesla was the original discoverer of so-called radio waves and invented the wireless to utilize these waves. But Tesla knew that the operation of radio waves depended upon ground currents and induction; therefore they were earthbound and their action extremely limited. When Tesla designed the set for interplanetary communications, he therefore avoided the use of radio waves. The set will not receive on any frequency used on earth. The small model that Mr. Matthews built is designed to receive from spaceships that are at least 5,000 miles above the surface of the earth and not more than 30,000 miles distant.

Mr. Matthews believes that our entire electrical system as used here on earth will not work beyond 8,000 miles out in space. However, when he first contacted spaceships on the Tesla set, the space people told him that our radio waves did not reach much beyond 5,000 miles, and that it is impossible to send a message on the present Tesla set from a spaceship more than 35,000 miles distant. Mr. Matthews has since started construction of a new set that is expected to provide a wider range, and he is incorporating many of his own discoveries in it, although it follows the basic Tesla design.

Tesla Scope

The interplanetary communications set is, however, only an interesting gadget. Like the telephone, it requires someone on the other end to make conversation; otherwise, it is simply connected with the silence of space. This set has no commercial value whatsoever, as the space people have no time to engage in idle chit-chat, and they are assuredly not in the entertainment business. They use the set only when they have an important message to give to Mr. Matthews and do not wish to take the time to land on his property and speak to him personally.

They explained to him in their very first conversation, that they had contacted him on the set because of his great faith in

Tesla, the Venusian they had brought to earth as a baby in 1856. They have, in recent years, made a world-wide survey to find out exactly what we have done with Tesla's inventions. They have also probed the depths of our hatred for each other, which is the main reason why most Tesla inventions have not been utilized, and they have reached the conclusion that, according to normal standards in this solar system, the entire population of the earth must be considered insane.

When the space people landed for a personal interview with Mr. Matthews, they were primarily interested in stimulating renewed activity in the Tesla anti-war machine. They found the Canadian location of the Matthews property ideal for the landing of their ships. They had previously given Mr. Matthews details of spaceship construction, size, shape, and so forth, in talks on the Tesla set.

Mr. Matthews has described his place in detail in his letters, and it does sound so delightful that it probably reminded the space people of our lovely, flower-decked globe that we enjoyed before the laggards came.

"Our place was originally an old Quebec farm," Mr. Matthews writes. "I love trees, so I planted many thousands of them to offer shelter, to attract the birds, and for their beauty alone. My little electrical shack is just that—a small rough building surrounded by trees; just like the hen in her nest, and just large enough to hold me, a desk, bench, books and tools.

"Besides this small shack we have the barn—really a barn —that we use for the larger stuff. But our real laboratory is the land, the open fields and sky; the mountain and the river. Here we study closely with God; it is wonderful what one can do when we walk with the Master!

"At one time we had a wonderful flower garden, but as the children grew up and got married off, and my lady and I traveled, we could not devote the necessary time to it: so at the moment we have a lovely garden of weeds, neck-high, but the flowers do shoot through the tangle. Besides, we have a lovely inside-the-house garden. You know—flower pots that keep me busy watering when their slave is away. Offhand, I cannot say how many flower pots there are, but they are plentiful!

"Anyhow, I use every bit of this property. In the winter I work in the old farmhouse that has stood here for over 200 years and which, like us, is old-fashioned. I have always been a tinkerer and always have something to fix for someone, from dolls to power plants. Then we must take time to listen to the wants and troubles of others, for there is always someone requiring help, which is our great joy to give, for this is our obligation to Him.

"In the early spring we start traveling, and most summers are spent this way, visiting and helping others. By faith I am a Christian Scientist, but let us always remember that Christ was and is the only true scientist.

"In this work concerning Tesla we must expect the materialistic world to be against us. That is our Cross, but be of good courage, for God never fails those who have faith in Him. Having a true understanding of God we can do anything so long as we serve as witnesses for the Christ. We have the supreme power of God on our side in preparing the world for the return of the Christ, and I believe spaceships have a great deal to do with it. There is nothing impossible, for Christ is with us, and the spirit of Tesla is with us. All we need is the will and courage to continue our present efforts. God will provide the wisdom and point the way.

"On my summer trips I take the Tesla set right along with me in case the space people wish to send through any messages. We combine business and pleasure on our long trips, for I usually do some research. We travel slowly and stop along the way to serve and help, and to share our knowledge with others, for that is a practical way of applying Divine Law and is far better than preaching.

"We do all kinds of work on these trips. We sketch, write, paint, consult, draw, lecture, hold prayer meetings, and help wherever we can. Nothing is either too big or too small, from fixing a radio, knitting a sock, or building a transmission line. Of course, we have a wonderful time and there is nothing like having God on the tow!

"I just draw for pleasure. I'm no expert and never had a lesson. I sketch, paint with oil, water, and colored pencil, from life, just to rest on the trips.

"I have been on earth a long time, so require some rest. I

drive slowly and never over three hundred miles a day, which is enough, considering that most of it is via Canada gravel. If I have any trouble I either fly or jump a train."

Mr. Matthews sent along some snapshots to us in the early days of our correspondence, so we knew that his description of his farmstead was indeed inadequate. But we were in no sense prepared for our first actual glimpse of the magnificent land of mountains and forests and open skies that greeted us on our first visit to this Canadian home.

It was autumn, and just at that moment of greatest loveliness when all Nature seems to hold its breath and say: "No, no, we cannot let this rapture fade. Let us hold this jewelled, this lighted moment forever! Let us breathe this wine-bright air; let us send forth our vision into the limitless blueness of space; let us dwell forever amid these jewel-tinted forests! Let us listen only to Wisdom spoken unto us by the Voice of Solitude!"

The Ships Arrive!

Then suddenly we were standing on historic ground—the great, sloping meadow that sweeps down from a forested mountain, aflame with autumn colors. "Here," said Mr. Matthews, "is where the ships land. This meadow, protected by the mountain at the back and the rise of ground at the front, forms a comfortable hollow in which the spaceships can nestle like birds."

He went on to explain that the first ship that came winging its way through the dark, moonless night, safe from prying eyes of the merely curious or the hostile, was a mother ship. "It was seven hundred feet in diameter," said Mr. Matthews, "three hundred feet high, with a center tube fifty feet in diameter. It held twenty-four small ships, each one from seventy-five to one hundred feet in diameter. None of the ships had windows as we know them, but the crew could obtain a full view on all sides by a device that somehow resembles television. The ship was of Venusian origin."

Mr. Matthews emphasized the fact that all his contacts, both on the set and personally, had been with real, living, material persons, not spirits. He does not hold with mediumship or communication with the dead, for he believes that we can all be in contact with God—the only true Spirit—through the living

Christ. He believes that all of us can receive comfort and other help from the Christ, and that only those who study spaceship information in the Bible and seek wisdom from God can ever understand the things of space.

It was thought at one time that Mr. Matthews might bring the Tesla set for interplanetary communication to New York and other cities and demonstrate it, but the space people informed him that such a demonstration would be useless at the present time. The doubters would still doubt, and even if they saw the machine and heard the messages they would still insist it was a trick of some sort. Apparently, there has not been much progress in these parts since the days of Joshua Coppersmith.

But there is another difficulty connected with bringing the Tesla set to New York. The set works on a very fine beam—finer than a hair, according to Tesla. The spaceships, flying at altitudes up to 25,000 miles, have worked out calculations whereby they can beam their signals to the set that is always in an exact location. The signal is not received if the set is moved even a few inches. Therefore, if the set is to operate in another city, it would be necessary to make prior arrangements with the space people, such as Mr. Matthews makes on his summer trips.

Furthermore, the space people do not warn Mr. Matthews when they wish to send their signals. He has rigged up an alarm on the set that rings if the spaceship is ready to send a message. If he is somewhere near the set, he hears the alarm and answers.

It can readily be seen that the operation of the set is entirely in the hands of the space people. They have requested Mr. Matthews not to give out information on the construction of the set at this time. The reason is that this type of willing service only encourages laziness among engineers and scientists who are quite capable of building a set if they would apply themselves, and as Mr. Matthews advocates—if they would attune their minds to God, as Tesla did.

Mr. Matthews has explained one basic idea that is not clear in the minds of the average person today. He emphasizes the fact that every radio and television set is a Tesla set. Therefore, an individual cannot have a clear understanding of electronics unless he has a clear understanding of Tesla's basic principles.

Mr. Matthews goes on to say that "no one apart from Tesla has ever made anything new in the way of a radio or television set—except for changes in design. The circuits, coils, condensers, and all important parts are all part of Tesla's basic discovery. So regardless of brand names, every set must be a Tesla set.

"However, the set for interplanetary communication is different both in the manner in which it operates, and because it is especially designed to receive signals from space. It is impossible to send ordinary radio waves through the upper layers above the earth. All such signals will bounce back to earth, as is well known to radio hams. Tesla knew this more than 50 years ago. He also knew that the space people would try to get in touch with us from their ships, so he devised this special machine that will receive their signals.

"Now due to the fact that the design was given to me by Tesla in confidence and in trust, to be used for the convenience of the space people when they approached the earth, I could not pass on this information to others without permission. The crew aboard the first space ship that landed on my property told me not to give out the information yet—which means that it can be made available at some time.

"Meanwhile the full directions for building the set can be found in the lectures that Tesla gave between the years of 1890 to 1896, and also in some other lectures that he gave in later years. What the space people desire is that someone in the United States discover the secret contained in the lectures, build a set, and then give full credit to Tesla.

"The 'dull?' Russians are rapidly discovering the lost secrets of Tesla, as they have demonstrated in producing the powerless aircraft Tesla invented for the United States at the close of World War I. But the Russians are giving Tesla full credit for the design.

"I do not know what Russia intends to do with the craft. Of course, the ship can carry the extra weight of bombs, and so forth, because there is no limit to the ground power plant, so it can be powered far beyond the ordinary plane. Besides the motor in the plane does not require any direct connection or fuel, so the craft is relieved of that weight. This machine was also reported in Tesla's old lectures, or at least the motor was described.

"The idea can also be adapted for both land and sea transportation. More than twenty years ago, I suggested that it be used to power our trains, and I wrote a paper for the magazine *Railway Electrical Engineer,* but nothing came of it.

"You see how small are the minds of the so-called experts. Here is all this information lying about, wide open to the public, and yet the big-wigs have to spend their time having fun with their space rockets. A number of these experts in both the United States and Canada have been trying to pump me for free information. They are too lazy and too dull to grasp Tesla's principles, so they want me to do all the brain work for them. But meanwhile the Russians are doing their own brain work, giving all due credit to Tesla, and coming up with his discoveries applied to industry.

"The point is that Americans have never used the information that Tesla gave them so freely, and now they are trying to pump me for more—probably with a view to robbing Tesla even further and making a few million for themselves. Nor does the pumping stop here. I have received letters from all over the world but they just do not have the right kind of bait to catch this fish. Money does not interest me, as it did not interest Tesla.

"Tesla was my lifelong friend and teacher. All I know concerning electrical engineering came from this wonderful man. He has always had first place in my thoughts, second only to God, and because of my faith in him all of my information concerning his discoveries and inventions is first hand. Many of his inventions, to my knowledge, have never been made public, and much of the confidential data that he gave me is not otherwise available. But until and unless these great experts, who are riding herd over us today, use the information which Tesla has made public, and give him full credit for it, it is useless to give them more....

"As recently as last night, one of our top scientists spent several hours with me. He did his best to obtain information on how true radar works, as conceived by Tesla in 1890. Well, I told him that it works without the use of reflectors, poles, towers, and so forth, and that it contained the germ of the idea that can explode all the atomic bombs on earth before they can even leave their home.

"But what these small-minded experts cannot realize is that Tesla designed radar as part of the anti-war machine. What the Americans are trying to do is to copy the Tesla system, of course, with no credit to him, but to use only the radar part for a defense against attack. If they used the entire anti-war machine, attack would become an immediate and permanent fact.

"This was known in 1935 when Tesla offered the anti-war machine to various governments. The heads of the allied governments then in power knew these facts and understood them. There was no excuse whatever for the Second World War. There is still no excuse for what is going on today.

"For these facts are still known among the great experts, but they are carefully concealed from the taxpayers—the little people who pay the bills for wars. A working model of the anti-war machine will cost about two million dollars, and it will include genuine radar—not the stuff the experts are fooling around with. Look what a mess they have made of it, trying to copy something from Tesla by stealing a part of his work, instead of adopting the anti-war machine outright.

"Millions are being spent on microwave towers for the so-called Distant Early Warning (DEW) lines, when according to Tesla not one pole, reflector or tower is needed. This is all utter waste. Even before the line was completed, even while it was still being designed, it was known that it would not be effective. Now the daily newspapers are coming out with a hint of the truth in headlines: Radar Defense Is Full of Holes. The whole thing is just another busted bubble, with millions of dollars wasted.

"That is why I will follow Tesla's instructions to the end. We certainly do not want any of these fine experts messing around with the anti-war machine. I had several letters from Tesla during his last days and as the information he sent me was confidential I intend to keep it that way.

"From first-hand information I know that Tesla did not leave any important notes for the authorities to find. Apart from his letters Tesla had other ways of communicating with me. The clique of big-wigs in the United States does not like this. Neither do the authorities, as I have discovered. When will people wake up and find that they can have no secrets from God?

"I could build Tesla's anti-war machine at any time, and could blow up all the atomic and H-bombs in the world. But of what use would that be? It would only destroy. It would not serve God. It would not help mankind. Peace can never come by man-made means of destruction imposed on humanity. So why try? Why bother? Peace can come only from the hearts of the people when their hearts are untroubled—when they really want to obey God and carry out His commands. The anti-war machine can be installed only when his people want it, in their hearts."

World Wireless System

"Another big waste today is in the television field. Not one of those tall TV towers is required. TV can be transmitted to any part of the world without any form of pole or tower, and this has been known since the turn of the century. The public assumes that all of this equipment is needed, but it is utter waste and is just used in order to provide bigger money profits. Any excuse is good enough, and the public is impressed when it sees all those big towers going up.

"It is the same with the World Wireless System for electrical distribution which Tesla invented. No poles, towers or wires are required. No expensive surveying. No useless manufacturing.

"The Tesla anti-war machine follows the same principle. It requires no poles, no lines, or large reflectors mounted on towers. Neither does it require an army to maintain it. It does provide positive protection for any coast line or national border. It is not, in any sense, a fence. The whole thing depends upon the "peaks" which are, of course, invisible to the human eye. All electric currents of whatever frequency pass in the earth and can be made to 'peak' or bounce up above the earth at regular measured distances.

"So far as the sputniks and other orbiting devices are concerned, these could not be designed to drop destruction on us from above if the Tesla anti-war machine was functioning. In addition to the protecting wall of light, the machine can also be built with a ceiling. If Tesla's machine is adopted, there is nothing that can affect it—nothing in the way of an A-bomb or H-bomb or any other bomb, even if it is transported on a missile, a rocket, or a sputnik.

"In the first place—and this is the important point—once Tesla's machine is set up, no form of bomb or high explosive can be made. In other words, if some nut tried to make a bomb and Tesla's machine was functioning, the bomb would explode right there, whether underground or in the air or any place else, and the nut would be blown to bits along with it."

No Atomic Bombs To Exist!

"So along with the adoption of the Tesla idea, no form of bomb or high explosive, such as an A-bomb or H-bomb, would continue to exist. For instance, if the United States decided to adopt Tesla's idea, she would notify all other countries of the date on which the switch would be thrown, giving them time to dump all forms of high explosives. Then on a certain date she would throw the switch. After that date, if any bombs existed, they would automatically explode. Even though some way could be discovered to protect the bombs temporarily—and that seems impossible—the moment someone tried to use them they would blow up, killing the user.

"But just supposing it might be possible for someone to send a missile with an H-bomb over the country. Of what use would it be? Simply to destroy? Because if the Tesla anti-war machine was in use, no such missile could enter the country. And after we saw the bomb coming, or even after it blew some of us up, we could still, from behind the wall of light, blow the enemy to bits and without the use of a single rocket.

"Rockets aimed at us would be useless, as would bombs in actuality, because anything would explode when it got within 200 miles of the wall, even if by some fantastic method it could be protected up to that point. So all these speculations really have no practical value, but they do help us to understand that Tesla thought of every possibility and prepared for every eventuality.

"Although Tesla himself loathed all deadly devices, nevertheless he knew that plenty of other people preferred war to God's peace. So when he designed the anti-war machine, he first worked out in detail all the possible weapons the machine might be called upon to destroy. He designed a jet-propelled airplane and an atomic bomb, the whole device radio-controlled, and able to cover a distance of 12,000 miles! And this was long ago. Tesla could easily look a hundred years into the future.

"In a letter which Tesla wrote to me in 1935, he said, speaking of his anti-war machine: 'My discovery ends the menace of airplanes, submarines, rockets or space machines, regardless of their height or speed. A century from now every nation will render itself immune from attack by my device.'

"I believe, as I believe in God, that the adoption of Tesla's machine will prevent war. Actually I have been fighting for Tesla since 1928, and have written hundreds of letters, newspaper and magazine articles about his inventions, so the world should know about this wonderful man."

Nikola Tesla, the author of 800 patented inventions.

Howard Menger's Electro-Craft X-1

Howard Menger was born on February 17, 1922 in Brooklyn, New York, and by the tender age of ten began to fully realize the vastness of the universe around him, something that obviously most youths can hardly contemplate much less on the scale that Howard did.

For it was early on that Menger—now retired and living in Florida—saw the bright shinning, circular objects skipping about the sky. In fact, one day along with his brother he witnessed a metallic object land not far from where they stood, but rather than being terrified as most of us would, he felt compelled to approach the object that, unfortunately, took off leaving him wondering who might be onboard.

Perhaps, as we look back at the situation, it was because of his curiosity and lack of fear that they later contacted him—*they* actually being an "exquisite woman with long golden hair which cascaded around her face and shoulders."

Right away Howard knew this woman could not have been born on this planet, as there was something totally different about her that set her apart from the rest of us. "She seemed," says Menger, "to radiate and glow as she sat on a rock before me, and I wondered if it were due to the unusual quality of the material she wore, which had a shimmering, shiny texture, not unlike but far surpassing the sheen of nylon."

Menger says the woman wore no makeup and her skin had pinkish undertones while her eyes were "opalescent discs of gold." When she spoke the first thing she said was, "Howard, we have come a long way to see you and to talk with you."

Thus began one of the most exciting cosmic adventures anyone could ever hope to have. It spanned many decades and included, Menger says, the opportunity to learn much in the way of scientific and technical data as revealed by beings from another world.

As it turns out, even though Menger tried to keep his contact with extraterrestrials as quiet as possible, he realized it was his duty to tell those willing to listen with open ears what he had found out regarding many of the subjects we have been taught, which have no basis in reality. For a period in the late 1950s and early 60s, Menger says that space ships were regularly landing in the back of his home in High Bridge, New Jersey. Supposedly, these human-in-appearance aliens would converse with Menger even in front of witnesses and from time to time would venture into his house to chat about everything from the proper diet, to ways in which to utilize the abundance of free energy that exists all around us.

"Those were fantastic times that I will never forget as long as I live," Menger reminisced. "The beauty and serenity of these beings was absolutely something to behold. It was almost as if you were speaking with one of God's angels."

Unfortunately as it often turns out, Howard may have found out—as well as spoke out—too much about flying saucers and extraterrestrials and therefore he had to pay the price. He found himself being harassed just as many other UFO witnesses and contactees do. There were the strange telephone calls in the middle of the night and the the visits by "agents" of an unknown origin warning him to keep silent.

Because he valued the safely of his family and friends as well as his own privacy, Menger began to back out of many of his public appearances. He had been a frequent guest on the highly popular Long John Nebel radio talk show broadcast nightly from Midnight to dawn over WOR radio in New York, but soon he refused to go on the air without any explanation. This despite the fact that he had written a book entitled *From Outer Space To You* that the publisher expected him to promote.

On national television one night, Menger went back on

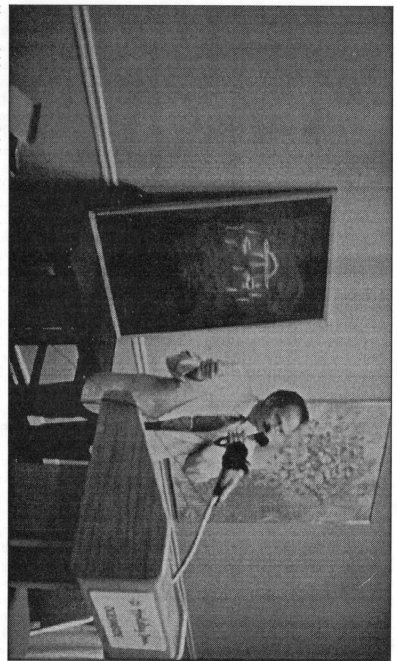

Howard Menger explaining electro-dynamic propulsion used in his electro-craft, which first flew successfully back in 1951.

everything he had said and in what seemed to be a shaky tone of voice confessed that things might not have been as he had thought. He seemed to say in so many words that there might not have been any extraterrestrials and that the government might have put him up to "inventing" such stories as a test to see how the public would relate to the landing of aliens.

After moving out of the area, Menger kept in hiding for many, many years, refusing to discuss the subject of UFOs even with former friends and associates. He said he had to get on with his life and that his business required his full attention (though he had several employees who seemed capable of doing the majority of the work).

It was not until the late summer of 1991 that what had actually happened to Howard Menger became more apparent. For the first time in nearly two decades, Howard and his charming wife, Connie, stood before an open microphone and addressed a huge throng of people who had crowded in to hear them speak as part of the third annual National New Age and Alien Agenda Conference in Phoenix, Arizona.

"The space people that I met explained much to me in the way of technology that they thought would improve our life down here on Earth." Menger explained that he had long tinkered with the concept of anti-gravity.

"From what I observed I thought that gravity might be a push instead of a pull. I realized that bodies in space, no matter what the size or speed they are travelling at, give off variable magnetic fields. This magnetic flux is an effect secondary to a primary cause which is the stream of energized particles coming from all directions in space and through all intervening bodies in space."

He recalled, in fact, one of his visitors telling him, "We take the energy from the atom, by removing the electron, and letting it go on its way. Nature puts it back into the atom without destroying anything; it's merely an exchange." One of the things which Howard discovered was that a tremendous amount of electrical energy, traveling in a circular or lineal motion close to the speed of light, could lift a craft off the ground.

As early as 1951—believe it or not—Menger built a craft

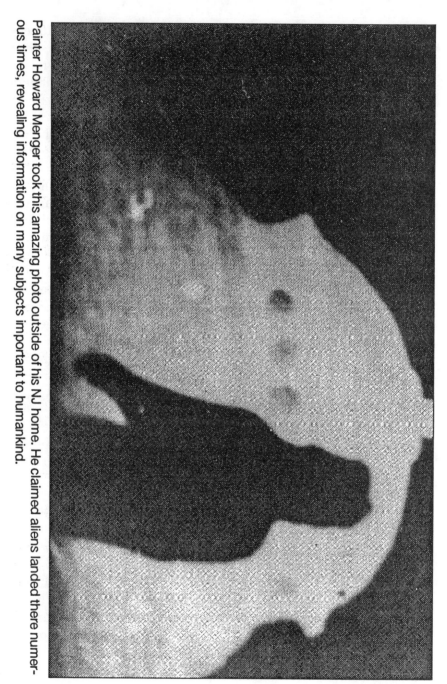

Painter Howard Menger took this amazing photo outside of his NJ home. He claimed aliens landed there numerous times, revealing information on many subjects important to humankind.

that not only took off, but flew hundreds of miles and was reported by witnesses as a real UFO when it finally crashed on the Pennsylvania-Ohio border.

"The craft, which we called the Electro-Craft X-1, cost me around $6,000 to construct," Menger recalls, with a slight hint of belated concern obvious in his voice.

"That was a lot of money to let fly away, especially in those days, and we couldn't figure out what had happened to the darn ship until two fellows came to our front door, identifying themselves as agents of the FBI. They said that the pieces of the craft were now in the hands of the government and warned us that it was illegal to fly any experimental craft over 500 feet without an FAA permit."

As it turned out, the FBI agents put Menger in touch with the "proper authorities" and the government did "aid and assist him in future development of his four-foot, radio-controlled, electro-craft. "To be frank," Menger confesses, "I was more interested in developing my propulsion system for ecological reasons, while they wanted it for the military." Menger says that his electro-dynamic propulsion system "would be environmentally safe, which is necessary if we are to bring about a peaceful humanity and become one with our galactic family."

Menger says he is willing to share his system with humanity, but needs funding. He would like to build and fly an Electro-Craft X-II, which would be a forty-foot in diameter flying saucer. Menger has recently published *The High Bridge Incident*, a large size book that sells for $23, and is available from him directly at: 845 28th Avenue, Vero Beach, Florida 32960.

Like Nikola Tesla before him, Howard Menger sees the future of Earth and all of humankind delicately balanced in the hands of some evil "super structure," who place their own welfare before that of the rest of us. "We need to change things, and we need to change them fast," Howard proclaims. "It's up to all of us to do our part."

And—indeed—we must all do our part before time runs completely out—which could be very soon!

This is a replica of a four foot radio controlled craft, built by Howard Menger in his sign and machine shop in New Jersey in 1951 (without toy soldiers). It was dubbed the X-1 electro-craft, after many successful test flights he lost radio contact at about 500 feet high, when it headed west and out of sight. Two weeks later, two men came to his shop with pieces, they said, were found on the Ohio–Pennsylvania border, where it crashed and was reported by some farmers to be a "ship from Mars." The two men, who said they were FBI, found him by tracing parts of the craft to electronic supply stores, etc., they warned him to keep quiet and not to do it again and that he would be contacted by an agency of the government in Washington, D.C., who were interested in the propulsion system and where he got it. A book, due soon, tells all! A 40 foot model is in the planning stage. Time of completion depends on investors and government grant.